THE PATH TO KNOWING GOD

THE PATH TO KNOWING GOD

LIVING OUT OUR GREATEST CALLING AND BLESSING

DEREK PRINCE

WHITAKER HOUSE

Publisher's Note:
This book was compiled from the extensive archive of Derek Prince's unpublished materials and approved by the Derek Prince Ministries editorial team.

Boldface type in the Scripture quotations indicates the author's emphasis. The forms *LORD* and GOD (in small caps) in Bible quotations represent the Hebrew name for God *Yahweh* (Jehovah), while *Lord* and *God* normally represent the name *Adonai*, in accordance with the Bible version used.

THE PATH TO KNOWING GOD:
Living Out Our Greatest Calling and Blessing

Derek Prince Ministries
P.O. Box 19501
Charlotte, NC 28219-9501
www.derekprince.org

ISBN: 979-8-88769-322-4
eBook ISBN: 979-8-88769-323-1
Printed in the United States of America

Whitaker House
1030 Hunt Valley Circle
New Kensington, PA 15068
www.whitakerhouse.com

Library of Congress Control Number: 2024943859

1 2 3 4 5 6 7 8 9 10 11 12 WH 31 30 29 28 27 26 25 24

"Knowing God in a personal relationship is the ultimate reason for our redemption."

—Derek Prince

CONTENTS

PART ONE: KNOWING OUR GOD

1. "The People Who Know Their God" 13
2. God's Purpose in Redemption 17
3. Keeping God's Covenant 27
4. The Power of Covenantal Relationships 31
5. Staying Centered 37
6. Our Need for Wisdom 43
7. Four Conditions for Knowing God 49
8. The Goal of Seeking 59
9. Into God's Presence 69

PART TWO: FULFILLING OUR DESTINY

10. Our Purpose in Life 81
11. Reigning with Christ 89

12. Our Forerunner......97
13. Our Pattern......107
14. Destined to Be Kings......117
15. Priests and Rulers Like Jesus......125
16. Ruling with Jesus's Authority......135
17. Ten Forces Opposing God......143
18. Carrying the Gospel of the Kingdom......151
About the Author......157

PART ONE:

KNOWING OUR GOD

"A desire to meet with God is the motivation that leads to the knowledge of God."
—Derek Prince

1

"THE PEOPLE WHO KNOW THEIR GOD"

After nearly sixty years of active involvement in the work of God in many nations, I have seen evil rise in the world at an alarming rate. The escalation of evil I have witnessed can only be described as cataclysmic. Dramatic changes in morality, relationships, and family life have resulted in an increase in violence, an upsurge in the divorce rate, and the open flaunting of wickedness in the form of sexually perverted lifestyles. When I look back at the upheaval I have seen, I ask myself, "Did all this happen in just a few years?"

We live in a period of incessant, violent, and uncontrollable change, a time about which Jesus prophesied that people's hearts will be "*failing them from fear*" (Luke 21:26). As we witness the decline coming on the earth, a pointed question arises within me: "Where will the people of God find the strength to stand in the midst of this rising tide of evil and to prevail against it? Where will they find the strength to stay true to their faith?"

STRONG PEOPLE

The world depicted at the close of the book of Daniel could just as well depict the world we are living in today; it is amazingly relevant to our times. Daniel's world was a place of increasing evil and opposition to God and His ways. This book of the Bible prophetically describes a time when evil will be tremendously powerful, sweeping away almost everything before it. In Daniel 11:32, we find the author referring to the evil *"king of the North"* (first mentioned in verse 6). However, in verse 32, Daniel also describes the *kind of person* who will not be overwhelmed by the flood of evil—one who will instead be active, successful, and triumphant in the midst of it:

> *Those who do wickedly against the covenant he shall corrupt with flattery; but the people who know their God shall be strong, and carry out great exploits.*

The *New International Version* says God's people *"will firmly resist"* (verse 32) this evil king. The Hebrew simply says they "shall do." That usage is like a blank check upon which *"the people who know their God"* can write anything. In other words, there is nothing believers will not be able to do. But here is the phrase that deserves our complete focus: *"The people who know their God* ***shall be strong.****"*

ULTIMATE SECURITY

Ultimately, the only secure source of strength and power available to any of us is the knowledge of God. Over many years, I have met Christians from just about every denomination and type in a variety of segments of the church. To my sorrow, most of them could not be described as strong.

My observation is that despite their interest in many subjects related to faith, most of God's people have relatively little time for God Himself. Now, there are always outstanding exceptions to that statement. But, basically, when you talk about power, people's ears open. When you talk about healing, they will come and listen to you almost endlessly. You can talk about other dramatic aspects of Christian ministry, and people are ready to receive. But I hear little that is being taught about God Himself, which makes me wonder if people are not interested in knowing Him. However, that focus is so important. Why? Because anything *not* rooted in God Himself will be swept away by the flood of evil rising in the world with each passing year. Again, a knowledge of God is our ultimate source of security and strength.

A lot of people, including some Christians, are hungry for power. But the mere desire for power can be extraordinarily dangerous. Swiss psychoanalyst Carl Jung said that the quest for power is a main motivation of human beings. Whether or not this is totally true, there is a hunger for power in almost every person, starting in early childhood. I believe that the desire for power is placed in humanity by the Creator Himself, because we were created to rule. (See Genesis 1:26–27.) But the problem is that unregenerate, fallen mankind wants power to rule without meeting the necessary conditions—the foremost of which is a personal relationship with our Creator.

These days, more than ever, we need to explore the essential subject of the knowledge of God, recognizing that genuine security is found only in knowing God personally. When we move into that awareness, we will discover God's true purpose in redemption, and we will live out our greatest calling and blessing. We will begin to become what He created us to be—a special people, a kingdom of priests, and a holy nation. This is God's very purpose in redeeming us, and it is the subject of this book.

2

GOD'S PURPOSE IN REDEMPTION

In the Old Testament account of the Israelites' deliverance from slavery in Egypt, God eventually led His people to the foot of Mount Sinai. It was there that He entered into a covenant with them and told Moses the purpose of Israel's redemption:

> *Thus you shall say to the house of Jacob, and tell the children of Israel: "You have seen what I did to the Egyptians, and how I bore you on eagles' wings and brought you to Myself. Now therefore, if you will indeed obey My voice and keep My covenant, then you shall be a special treasure to Me above all people; for all the earth is Mine. And you shall be to Me a kingdom of priests and a holy nation."*
>
> (Exodus 19:3–6)

WHAT *WE* CAN'T AFFORD TO MISS

The brief passage from Exodus 19 above outlines what God intended Israel's destiny to be. Unfortunately, this is the very lesson that Israel missed—and what, I believe, Christians today are in equal danger of missing.

Through His miraculous power—*"I bore you on eagles' wings"* (verse 4)—God redeemed Israel from Egypt. The next phrase in that verse is the lesson they failed to grasp: *"and brought you to Myself."* This is the essential point we can't afford to miss: *God redeemed the Israelites primarily to bring them to Himself.*

In the Hebrew language, the phrase translated *"to Myself"* is the shortest possible word: *el*. Many Jewish people miss this tiny word when reading Scripture. Even though the phrase in English is longer, multitudes of Christians, as I mentioned earlier, are also in danger of missing it. God's primary purpose in redemption was—and is—to bring His people to Himself. Why? So that we may know Him. Everything else is secondary.

For the most part, God's purpose for Israel as revealed in Exodus 19 was never fulfilled. Certain individuals in the Bible, like David and Daniel, grasped and fulfilled their callings. But, overall, Israel never realized the purpose of her redemption. Perhaps that is why God had the apostle Peter restate that purpose for the church. In his first New Testament letter, Peter applied God's words from Exodus 19:6 to all who believe in Jesus Christ: *"You are a chosen generation, a royal priesthood, a holy nation, His own special people"* (1 Peter 2:9). Thus, these words apply not only to Israel after her redemption from Egypt but also to believing Christians today. You and I need to give special heed to what God is saying about our calling in Him! (This will be our focus in later chapters.)

One lesson from Israel's failure is that Satan can delay the outworking of God's purpose. But the good news for us is that the enemy can never ultimately prevent it. If God's purpose is not accomplished the first time, He does not give up and say, "Well, I guess Satan won that one." He waits until He finds those who will cooperate with His purpose.

What God intends to be done *will* be done. The question is not whether it will be done but *by whom*. Here is the pointed question for us: Will we discover our destiny in God? Or will we make the same mistake Israel made, never fully comprehending or fulfilling God's basic purpose of redemption?

HOW TO DRAW CLOSE

How do you and I draw close enough to the Lord to understand and walk in His purpose for us? There are two basic requirements for us, illustrated again by God's dealings with Israel.

In Exodus, we see that God goes on to speak about His covenant, giving Israel the law and ultimately the promise of a land to inherit. The Jewish people were excited about the law. Even for Orthodox Jews today, the one word that dominates their thinking is *Torah*, the Hebrew word for *Law*. Definitely, Jewish people today are also interested in the land. But I find few anywhere who are excited about knowing God. It is as if they have gone for the product and are scarcely aware of God Himself—even though bringing the Israelites to Himself, as we have seen, was God's primary purpose in redeeming Israel.

In every age and dispensation, God has two requirements for His redeemed people that are basic for a relationship with

Him. God's message to Moses in Exodus 19 identifies these two requirements:

> *Now therefore, if you will indeed* ***obey My voice*** *and* ***keep My covenant....*** (verse 5)

In the remainder of this chapter, we will examine the first of these requirements: *obey God's voice*. Throughout the books of Exodus and Deuteronomy, God repeats this first requirement consistently: "*Obey My voice*." Could His requirement be any clearer or any simpler?

HEARING AND OBEYING

In Deuteronomy 28, there are sixty-eight verses that outline in great detail the blessings and curses promised to the nation of Israel—fourteen verses of blessings and fifty-four verses of curses. The condition for experiencing either one or the other—blessings or curses—is simple:

> *If you diligently obey the voice of the* Lord *your God, to observe carefully all His commandments...all these blessings shall come upon you and overtake you, because you obey the voice of the* Lord *your God.... But it shall come to pass, if you do not obey the voice of the* Lord *your God, to observe carefully all His commandments and His statutes which I command you today, that all these curses will come upon you and overtake you.* (Deuteronomy 28:1–2, 15)

The list of blessings that follow in verses 3–13 include God's favor, health, reproductiveness, prosperity, protection, victory, and exaltation, to name just a few. In contrast, the list of curses—the result of disobeying God's voice—is horrible! Verses 15–68 of Deuteronomy 28 outline all manner of spiritual, emotional, physical, relational, and financial problems. Why do these curses come? Here again, the reason is simple: *"You do not obey the voice of the* L*ORD your God"* (verse 15).

What happened when Israel *did* obey the voice of the Lord? God blessed her for it. The primary condition for receiving the blessing is listening to the voice of the Lord and then doing what He says. If we do not hear His voice, we cannot know what He is telling us to do. But in listening to His voice, we must also listen with an attitude of being willing to obey what He tells us to do.

In a very real sense, the destiny of each of us is determined by the conditional word *if*: *"If you diligently heed the voice of the* L*ORD your God and do what is right in His sight"* (Exodus 15:26). My observation is that most people who *"diligently heed"* His voice also do what is right. By contrast, those who don't do what is right are most often the ones who don't listen to Him. For you and me, the course our lives take will be decided by whether we diligently hear and heed the voice of the Lord our God. How we listen determines our destiny.

MAINTAINING FOCUS

Unfortunately, not many Christians seem to have the determination or single-minded focus required to hear and obey. I'm always amazed at how people tend to bypass the primary focus and become distracted by secondary priorities. Most religious people—including, but not limited to, Christians—get so taken up with the means (often, their particular way of doing things) that they lose sight of the ends that the means were designed to achieve. A means is something you do in order to achieve an end. An end is something worthwhile for its own sake.

The New Testament identifies two great ends, or results, of obeying—pursuits that are valuable in themselves. It so happens that, in the English language, each of these pursuits ends with the suffix *ship*: *fellowship* and *worship*. All church activity that does not bring people into these two experiences is vain—wood, hay, and stubble, which will be burned up on the day of judgment. (See 1 Corinthians 3:12–13.)

RECOGNIZING HIS VOICE

True followers of the Lord focus on the primary goal—the end—rather than secondary priorities, which may not have lasting value. This is made plain not only in the old covenant, but also in the new. Yet this simple truth about hearing and obeying God comes as a surprise to some Christians.

Jesus stated succinctly and clearly who His true disciples are. He did not name any group, denomination, or doctrinal persuasion but simply said, *"My sheep hear My voice, and I know them, and they follow Me"* (John 10:27). In other words, Jesus's true disciples are the ones who hear His voice and do what He says. The picture here is of an Eastern shepherd who does not drive his sheep, goading and prodding the animals from behind, but instead leads them by the sound of his voice. When the sheep recognize the shepherd's voice, they follow him. Jesus was saying, "If you want to be one of My sheep, you must listen, recognize My voice, and act on what I tell you."

Notice that Jesus does not say, "My sheep read the Bible." Please don't misunderstand me. Reading the Bible is very important. However, it is possible to read the Word without hearing the voice of the Shepherd. Reading the Bible, in itself, is not sufficient. Jesus said, *"My sheep hear My voice."* What does that signify? Personal relationship.

Nothing is more distinctive in a personality than the voice. When my wife phones me, I know who is calling as soon as I hear her voice. Why? Because I know my wife. If you and I know a person, we recognize that person's voice. If you and I do not recognize someone's voice, it is questionable whether we really know the person.

DILIGENTLY HEEDING

The rest of Exodus 15 reinforces the kind of determination to hear and obey that we have been discussing. Verse 26 says:

> *If you diligently heed the voice of the* Lord *your God and do what is right in His sight,...I will put none of the diseases on you which I have brought on the Egyptians. For I am the* Lord *who heals you.*

What is the first condition for having the Lord as our "Doctor" who heals us? Diligently heeding. *"If you diligently heed the voice of the* Lord *your God and do what is right in His sight."* Once again, the condition is obedience.

God was making Himself available as Israel's Physician. Israel did not ask for this; it was a sovereign revelation of God. (Let me say here that anyone who turns down the offer of the Lord's services as personal Physician is unwise.) There is another aspect to the phrase *"I am the* Lord *who heals you"* that relates to our decision to make the Lord our Physician. The above statement is in the continuous present tense: "I am the Lord who is healing you." If you are living in contact with the Lord, He is healing you all the time. It is a continual process.

"LISTEN LISTENING"

The meaning in the Hebrew for the first requirement—*"If you diligently heed the voice of the* L*ORD your God"* (Exodus 15:26)—indicates you must "listen listening." In the Hebrew language, the most emphatic way to express a verb is to double it or say it twice. God is therefore emphasizing this truth about heeding by saying, "If you will *listen listening.*"

I began to study the theme of healing in the Bible when I was hospitalized in North Africa during World War II, being treated by doctors who were unable to cure me. I had just come to faith in the Lord Jesus, and I realized that if I were to get out of the hospital, it would have to be God's doing. So, I decided to read through the entire Bible and underline in blue everything related to four topics: healing, health, physical strength, and long life. It took me several months, but in the end, do you know what I had? A blue Bible! What impressed me most of all was the fact that *healing depends on listening to God.*

Having conducted many healing services since then, I have concluded that most Christians seeking healing are really just asking for a little patch of God's supernatural blessing to sew onto the old clothes of their Christian walk. But Jesus said, *"No one puts a piece of unshrunk cloth on an old garment"* (Matthew 9:16). Most people want healing, but they are not prepared to revolutionize their walk with the Lord. If you begin to listen to the Lord, however, your life *will* be radically changed. I could fill this entire book with the revolutionary blessings that result from listening to the voice of the Lord.

Remember that the Hebrew says, "If you will *listen listening.*" As I lay in my hospital bed and pondered this fact, I asked myself, "What does it mean to 'listen listening'?"

I sensed the Lord giving me this answer: *You have two ears, a right ear and a left ear. To listen listening is to listen to Me with your right ear and your left ear—not listen to Me with your right ear and to something else with your left ear.* After I *listened listening* to God, I was released from the hospital. In later chapters, I will share more about this experience and how it applies to the blessings of knowing God.

3

KEEPING GOD'S COVENANT

In the previous chapter, we examined the first requirement for embracing the purpose of God for our lives: listening to the voice of the Lord and then doing what He says. In this chapter, we will cover the next step in the process.

The second requirement for God's redeemed people to deepen their relationship with Him appears in Exodus 19:5, immediately after the first one: "*Now therefore, if you will indeed obey My voice and keep My covenant....*" Thus, the second basic requirement is *to keep God's covenant.*

THE BASIS OF RELATIONSHIP

It is interesting to note that in both the Hebrew of the Old Testament and the Greek of the New Testament, the word translated as *covenant* (in Hebrew, *briyth,* and in Greek, *diatheke*) can also be translated as *testament.* It is good for us to recognize that when we read the Old Testament and the New Testament, we are actually reading the old covenant and the new covenant. This is significant because the whole of God's Word comes to us in the form of two covenants.

God has no favorites. He blesses those who, first of all, hear and obey His voice, and then, second, keep His covenant. God enters into a permanent relationship only on the basis of a covenant. The moment He intends to have an enduring, permanent relationship with anyone, He establishes a covenant with them. It is in covenant that we can truly come to know God. That covenant determines the grounds of the relationship and the responsibilities on either side—God's side and our side. These requirements are set up like a legal document.

THE PLACE OF SACRIFICE

One other truth concerning covenant is that it is always based on a sacrifice. I made this discovery in a remarkable way during the closing years of World War II. I had become a believer by this time and was stationed in the Middle East in what was then called Palestine. I decided to teach myself Hebrew by reading the Bible in Hebrew with the English version alongside. I started where anybody would start: in Genesis.

Using the methodology I had implemented in the hospital in North Africa (where I ended up with the blue Bible), I began underlining certain themes of Scripture in different colors. This time, using my Hebrew Bible, I decided to underline three themes: covenant, sacrifice, and the shedding of blood.

Covenant was blue, sacrifice was green, and the shedding of blood was, logically, red. I was not even halfway through the book of Genesis when I realized that every time there was a covenant, a sacrifice was made. Correspondingly, every time a sacrifice was made, there had to be the shedding of blood. These great basic truths, if we can grasp them, will help us to enter into a relationship with God: a sacrifice always means a life laid down, evidenced by shed blood. Thankfully, the sacrifice for us to enter into covenant with God was made when Jesus's blood was shed on our behalf on Calvary. (See, for example, Luke 22:20.)

COVENANT IN MARRIAGE

This principle of covenant holds true in God's design for marriage. A biblical marriage is a covenant designed by God between a man, a woman, and God Himself. Two people enter a covenant through sacrifice, each laying down their life for the other, each finding fulfillment and achievement in the life of the other. A life laid down is the essence of God's design for marriage.

When a marriage is not understood as a covenant, it almost invariably disintegrates. Most men and women today have lost the concept of marriage as a covenant. Many people choose to live together outside of marriage. Of those who do marry, there is in most Western nations a divorce rate of around 50 percent. Until the concept of covenant is restored, the institution of marriage will continue to break down, even among Christians.

A successful marriage does not depend on whether you belong to a church or are religious. It doesn't depend upon your being a good person. Here is the key factor: are you both meeting God's condition in that covenant with a life laid down for the sake of the other?

COVENANT IN THE CHURCH

Alongside the validity of this principle for marriage, covenant applies to any permanent relationship in the kingdom of God. In each case of relationship, there must be a covenant with a life laid down. The covenant that unites the body of Christ was made through the blood of Jesus. If Jesus *"laid down His life for us,"* says the apostle John in 1 John 3:16, we must also lay down our lives for one another.

A church flounders when it is made up of people who do not lay down their lives for one another. They may have correct theology and follow all sound practices of Christian living, church leadership, and moral discipline. But if they are not laying down their lives for one another, ultimately, their theology and principles will not keep them together.

In 1963, I was deeply impacted by Watchman Nee's book *The Normal Christian Church Life*. When I started reading it, I thought I was going to discover the outline of the perfect church. Of course, the problem is that there is no such thing as a perfect church. It is often said that if we ever do discover the perfect church, we should not join it, because then it would no longer be perfect! This is true. But the key to building a church according to God's blueprint is using the right materials. If an architect were to design a building based on using reinforced concrete, and all the contractor had was lumber, the building could not be built. Our problem in the church is not the blueprint; it is the materials. The materials essential for building the church are covenantal relationships in which we lay our lives down for one another, as we will further explore in the following chapter.

4

THE POWER OF COVENANTAL RELATIONSHIPS

We have seen the vital nature of covenants—first and foremost, in our relationship with God, but also in marital relationships and in relationships between believers. Each of these covenants, if entered into as God intended, helps us to deepen our knowledge of Him and His ways. In this chapter, we will continue to explore what it means to be in covenantal relationship with God and with our fellow believers in the church.

Ephesians 4 is the great church-building chapter; in verse 11, it lists all five building ministries: apostles, prophets, evangelists, pastors, and teachers. However, many people miss the foundational truths for these ministries found in the first three verses of Ephesians 4:

> *I, therefore, the prisoner of the Lord, beseech you to walk worthy of the calling with which you were called, with all*

> *lowliness and gentleness, with longsuffering, bearing with one another in love, endeavoring to keep the unity of the Spirit in the bond of peace.* (Ephesians 4:1–3)

NOT JUST HEAD KNOWLEDGE

An essential part of laying down our lives for one another in covenant—which is also the basis for sound ministry—is *humility*. You cannot build a church according to God's blueprint without humble people. Too often, we believe we need to give people more knowledge. But what does knowledge do? *"Knowledge puffs up, but love edifies"* (1 Corinthians 8:1). Please note that we are speaking here of head knowledge that does not lead to a deeper relationship with God or apply to our daily lives.

Imparting knowledge alone is the shortsighted goal of many seminaries—one that does not produce healthy churches. If you take young men and women and put a lot of theological information into their heads, they tend to become puffed up. They emerge from seminary with little practical experience, thinking they know all the answers. Many who are puffed up with knowledge are unwilling to acknowledge that they do not know the basic, practical truths of the New Testament.

Many of the major problems of the church today can be traced back to the "new theology" that emanated from Germany toward the end of the 1800s. This core teaching has now infected much of the professing church, particularly in Europe and the United States. Whenever believers deny the truth of Scripture and the person of the Holy Spirit—which the church in Germany officially rejected with a document signed by pastors in the early 1900s—it inevitably opens the way for the next most powerful force in the universe: the spirit of Antichrist.

LOYAL AND FAITHFUL

The essence of covenant, then, is not theological knowledge but personal or relational knowledge. Much of the evangelical church today has unintentionally misrepresented what it means to believe in Jesus Christ. "Believing" has come to mean adhering to a set of Bible verses or accepting a theological system. In the Old and New Testaments, however, in both Hebrew and Greek, the word for a believer describes an aspect of character, not intellect. This character trait may be summed up in one of two words: *loyal* or *faithful*.

A faithful person is a loyal person. Habakkuk 2:4 says, "*The just shall live by his faith.*" In other words, the just man or woman will live by their loyalty to God—even in the midst of disasters such as all those described in the book of Habakkuk. The just person will live in the midst of these trials because of their commitment to God.

God requires, first and foremost, loyalty to Himself. After that comes loyalty to His covenantal people. Jesus summed it up in this way: "'*You shall love the* Lord *your God with all your heart, with all your soul, and with all your mind.' This is the first and great commandment. And the second is like it: 'You shall love your neighbor as yourself.' On these two commandments hang all the Law and the Prophets*" (Matthew 22:37–40). In terms of the Bible, then, a person disloyal to God is not a believer. Loyalty is the key to understanding covenant.

BREAKING BREAD

In the sacrament of Communion, breaking bread is the outward evidence of our covenant with God and with His people. When we take Communion, we are committing ourselves, among other things, to be loyal to the body of Christ. It is a terrible sin to walk out of a Communion service and then start to speak against the very people with whom we have just broken bread—we have become covenant-breakers. There is nothing more serious in the Bible than being a covenant-breaker.

The significance of breaking bread is graphically illustrated in the book *O Jerusalem!* This work, written by two journalists, recounts what happened in Jerusalem during 1947–1948 when the State of Israel was being born. I was an eyewitness to much of what happened during that time, and I can vouch for the basic accuracy of the book.

The authors, Larry Collins and Dominique Lapierre, describe an incident that took place in a Jewish settlement south of Jerusalem that had been overrun by the Arab Legion of Jordan. Most of the Jewish defenders had been killed. But among a handful who survived was a young Jewish woman from Poland. When the Arab soldiers captured her, and two of them began to tear her clothes off to rape her, an amazing thing happened. The Arab officer in command—a Muslim, without a doubt—decided to stop them. He walked up to them, right in front of bystanders, drew his revolver, and shot both of the soldiers dead. Then he pulled a piece of bread out of his pocket, handed it to the Jewish woman, and said, "Eat this." When she had eaten it, he said, "Now you're safe. No one will touch you. You have broken bread with me."[1]

When I read of that incident in this powerful book, I thought to myself, "If only Christians understood as much as Muslims do about what it means to break bread."

1. Larry Collins and Dominique Lapierre, *O Jerusalem!* (New York: Simon & Schuster, 1988), 364.

I hope it has become clear from this chapter that humility and loyalty are essential elements of a covenantal relationship with God and others. As we commit to developing these qualities, we will enter more fully into the knowledge of God.

5

STAYING CENTERED

In this chapter, which is somewhat of a review of our first few chapters, we return to the primary theme we are exploring in this book: knowing God personally is our greatest calling and blessing, through which we find true security. When we move into that awareness, we will discover God's ultimate purpose in redemption. We will begin to become what He created us to be—a special people, a kingdom of priests, and a holy nation. As Exodus 19:5–6 tells us:

> *Now therefore, if you will indeed obey My voice* ["listen listening"] *and keep My covenant, then you shall be a special treasure to Me above all people; for all the earth is Mine. And you shall be to Me a kingdom of priests and a holy nation.*

We see that God's promise to Israel stated in these verses has three aspects:

1. Israel will be a special people.
2. Israel will be a kingdom of priests.
3. Israel will be a holy nation.

Each of the three facets of this promise from Exodus 19 is restated in 1 Peter 2:5, 9:

> *You also, as living stones, are being built up a spiritual house, a holy priesthood, to offer up spiritual sacrifices acceptable to God through Jesus Christ.... You are a chosen generation, a royal priesthood* [a kingdom of priests], *a holy nation, His own special people.*

GOD'S UNCHANGING PURPOSE

God's purpose, as we can clearly see from the verses above, has not changed! He continues looking for a people who will fulfill His destiny for them. The Lord will wait thousands of years, if necessary. He is patient to see His will accomplished in all things.

I am deeply convinced, from observing my own life and the lives of others, that if God says He will do something, we can be absolutely sure He will do it. As my friend Bob Mumford has said, "God has a bulldozer. When He turns His bulldozer loose, anything that stands in its way—no matter what it is—will be razed." Certainly, God is merciful and gracious. But He is also relentless. Wisdom dictates that we acknowledge His bulldozer and let Him accomplish His purpose in us. Why? Because you and I cannot stop it, run away from it, or turn aside from it.

Let's return to another foundational verse we reviewed in chapter 2: Exodus 19:4, in which the Lord said to Israel,

You have seen what I did to the Egyptians, and how I bore you on eagles' wings and brought you to Myself.

Again, even before the Lord sets forth any conditions or promises in later verses, He reveals His ultimate intention. We have seen that God's primary objective in redemption is to bring us to Himself. Tragically, most of God's people, whether Jewish or Christian, have never really understood the amazing depth of this statement. God's primary desire is not to bring us into a covenant, a law, or even a promised land. *It is to bring us to Himself.* This is His deepest longing and firmest purpose. Truthfully, it is the only place of true safety in the world. Let us always remember that ultimate security is found through a deep, intimate, personal relationship with the Lord Himself.

AVOIDING "GOD PLUS SOMETHING"

As we observed earlier, many people in the church today bypass a personal relationship with the Lord. Instead, they are distracted or preoccupied with some secondary pursuit. They may be able to quote Scripture and discuss doctrine, especially if they have a particular agenda. Sometimes, regardless of what you try to talk with them about, they always bring the topic back to their own specific focus. It's unfortunate because, that way, they are missing the primary purpose of their redemption—which, as we are learning, is to know the Lord.

Some of us may get all wrapped up in going to church, knowing the Bible, seeking miracles, or even advancing evangelism. Those are all good pursuits, but if we are not primarily wrapped up in God, we are missing the central purpose of our salvation. When we bypass knowing God, we miss everything. God will still bless us and help us. But we will not enter into His purpose for us. If you and I could hear the sounds of heaven, we would hear a deep sob in the heart of the Lord. He would be saying, "They want everything I have to offer, but they are not interested in knowing Me."

This was true of me. As a professional philosopher, I searched everywhere (except for the right place—God) for the answer to life's problems. Earlier in life, I had concluded that Christianity was not the answer, so I turned to Greek philosophy, to yoga, and to all sorts of other outlandish ideas. Finally, late one night in 1941 in an army barracks room, when no one else was awake, I had a personal encounter with the Lord Jesus Christ. In that encounter, I met the Answer.

Later, I read in Colossians about Jesus Christ, "*in whom are hidden all the treasures of wisdom and knowledge*" (Colossians 2:3). I said to myself, "Why should I grub around any longer in the rubbish bins of human wisdom when all the treasures are hidden in Jesus Christ?" The Bible, I decided, is the Book with the answers, and I wanted to find in its pages what God has hidden in Jesus Christ. Everything I had tried to find in philosophy and in human wisdom I now found in Him.

Since then, I have been deflected and diverted on occasion into side issues. But, thankfully, I have always returned to this truth: Jesus is "*the Alpha and the Omega, the Beginning and the End, the First and the Last*" (Revelation 22:13), "*the author and finisher of our faith*" (Hebrews 12:2). In fact, it is a sacrilege for anyone to put Jesus Christ on the same level with Buddha, Socrates, Muhammad, or anyone or anything else.

FINDING THE ANSWER

One unfortunate deterrent to knowing God personally is an attitude I call "God plus something." Different groups have their different "somethings." They believe that God plus something will do the job for them. No, *God* will do the job—never mind about the "something." When we have God, we don't need anything or anyone else to amplify that vital relationship. These "God-plus-something" people ought to go to the book of Colossians. That is where Paul clearly states that Jesus Christ is the final answer:

> *In Him dwells all the fullness of the Godhead bodily; and you are complete in Him, who is the head of all principality and power.* (Colossians 2:9–10)

Jesus is the only answer. We are *"complete in Him."* We do not need God plus anything else.

Whenever anyone starts to look outside of Jesus Christ, they will discover a multitude of fascinating and exciting theories and doctrines. But, ultimately, they will find, like the prodigal son, that they are feeding on husks when they could be living on the Father's bread! (See Luke 15:11–32.)

Once more, for any of us as believers, it is possible to know the Bible inside and out, to read stacks of inspirational books, to attend conferences year after year, hearing the best preachers in the world, but still miss the mark. What should be your true objective? What is the supreme experience to fulfill the purpose for which God redeemed you? *The knowledge of God Himself.* Knowledge of anything else—no matter how good or right—will never satisfy the deepest desires of your heart. Only a personal relationship with God Himself through His Son, Jesus Christ, will accomplish this.

So, if you find yourself inclined to study the philosophies of human beings to find the ultimate answer for your life, I would advise you to check your motives. What are you searching for? Are you seeking more knowledge *about* God? Or are you seeking a personal relationship *with* God? Take the opportunity *now* to set the personal knowledge of God as your highest pursuit. Once you know Him personally, you are on your way to finding true security. Only then will you fulfill His purpose for your life.

6

OUR NEED FOR WISDOM

As expressed in the previous chapters, knowing God in a personal relationship is the ultimate purpose of our redemption. The cry of the apostle Paul was, "*That I may know Him*" (Philippians 3:10). Even if you know all kinds of wonderful details and facts, if you do not know God, you have missed everything! Let's ask ourselves again: Is it our heart's desire to know Him in all His fullness?

TRUE WISDOM

The book of Proverbs offers tremendous insight on how to find the knowledge of God. The second chapter of Proverbs is especially meaningful to me, and I find myself returning to it regularly in my study of this topic.

> *My son* [or "my daughter," since the Hebrew encompasses both sexes], *if you receive my words, and treasure*

> *my commands within you, so that you incline your ear to wisdom, and apply your heart to understanding; yes, if you cry out for discernment, and lift up your voice for understanding, if you seek her as silver, and search for her as for hidden treasures; then you will understand the fear of the* Lord, *and find the knowledge of God.* (Proverbs 2:1–5)

Moving ahead a few verses, we read:

> *When wisdom enters your heart, and knowledge is pleasant to your soul, discretion will preserve you; understanding will keep you.* (verses 10–11)

Clearly, the emphasis of the first eleven verses of Proverbs 2 is *wisdom.*

THREE ASPECTS OF WISDOM

Some years ago, the Lord showed me my need for each of the three aspects of wisdom mentioned in Proverbs 2: *understanding, insight,* and *discretion.* As I turned to the Hebrew and studied these three words, I made some interesting observations, which I share with you now.

1. UNDERSTANDING

The best way to describe *understanding* is by the English word *comprehension.* In Latin, "to comprehend" means "to take in the whole of a thing; to get an overall perspective." To understand is to be able to see a situation as a whole.

As believers with understanding, for example, you and I can look at current events and see God's purposes being worked out and His prophetic word being fulfilled. Or we can look at a situation in a church and see the whole situation, in all its elements—how they relate and where the problems are. Having understanding in a marriage would mean seeing all the different factors in the relationship, the root problems, the sources of those problems, and why the marriage might be in danger of breaking down. So, again, understanding is the ability to see the whole picture.

2. INSIGHT

As I continued my study, I learned that *insight* means the ability to see into situations and to have discernment. Actually, another word for *insight* is *discernment*. To *discern* is "to recognize and distinguish between things or people."

If you and I have insight, we are no longer just looking at a mass of people in a church; we are seeing and recognizing the different aspects of each individual there. For example, we may discern the various degrees of commitment and loyalty among those gathered, or the different agendas people have for relating to one another. Or, as described previously, we may be able to look at a married couple and recognize what may be causing problems between them. One aspect of insight is a gift the Bible calls *"discerning of spirits"* (1 Corinthians 12:10). This is the capacity to recognize spirits and distinguish between them, identifying whether or not they are from God.

3. DISCRETION

Discretion, the third aspect of wisdom, is a very interesting term. The Hebrew word is *mezimmah*, which comes from a root word meaning "to plan or to plot." In the Old Testament, this term is often used in a negative context with regard to a plan or a plot, such as in Psalm 10:2: *"Let them be caught in the plots which they have devised."* However, it is also used in a positive sense at times—and it is even used in relation to God Himself. When God has given you understanding and insight, then He gives you *discretion*—the knowledge of what to do with your understanding and insight.

Unfortunately, the area of discretion is where many of us slip up. We may clearly see the truth about someone or something, but seeing is not enough. If I were to describe *discretion* in New Testament words, they would be the words of Jesus: "*Be as shrewd as snakes and as innocent as doves*" (Matthew 10:16 NIV, BSB). In a certain sense, we need to be shrewd. Many relational problems at home, at church, and in society would be avoided if we used greater discretion in what and how we communicated with one another.

Basically, discretion is knowing what to say about certain truths, as well as when and how to say it—and, just as importantly, when *not* to say it.

A LIFE LESSON

In the period when I was focusing my study on these three aspects of wisdom—understanding, insight, and discretion—I asked God to reveal them to me more fully. What followed that prayer was a unique experience for me. It happened at a time when my wife Ruth and I were hosting a group of Americans on a tour to Israel with the help of an Israeli tour guide. During one of our teaching sessions, I was giving a talk on Israel. In the tour audience was a man who happened to be a professional psychiatrist. He was not a particularly "spiritual" person, and this actually made it more significant to trust what God showed him, as opposed to someone who would approach the topic solely from a spiritual perspective.

This gentleman, somewhat reluctant to talk with me, approached the Israeli tour guide. The psychiatrist told the guide that, while I was speaking, he had seen three heads behind me, from my right to my left. At first, he thought he was seeing things, so he blinked, closed his eyes, and looked again. But the heads were still there. He was totally unaware that he was receiving a spiritual revelation.

The tour guide found me and shared what this man had seen. The moment he began to describe it, I thought, "God is telling me something." So, I went to the psychiatrist himself and said to him, "Tell me what you saw."

"The first head, I saw very clearly," he said. "It was well-formed and very distinct. It was a bearded head with a firm expression, and it seemed to have authority. I couldn't tell whether the second one was a man or a woman because it wasn't as clear. It seemed to be wearing something like a cloak or a cowl or a hood. The third head I could hardly see at all because it was very unclear."

"What were they doing?" I asked.

"They reminded me of the Secret Service agents who guard the president when he is making an appearance," he replied. "They were watching earnestly for anything that would threaten you."

I thought, "God, how good You are! I never even knew these guardians were there."

Remembering my prayer to know more about the three aspects of wisdom, I understood that these were the three benefits I had been praying for—understanding, insight, and discretion. God was showing me a fuller picture of their roles in my life. The "head" with the beard on my right, I knew, was *understanding.* He was clear, firm, and authoritative. What God was revealing to me was that I had a solid degree of understanding.

The less-defined figure in the middle represented *insight.* It was interesting that it could be either male or female, because insight is often considered to be just as much a feminine trait as a masculine one. (Like me, most husbands would probably agree that their wife usually has more insight than they have.) The Lord was showing me that insight was present in my life, but it was not fully formed.

Then, on my left, was *discretion,* which was the least distinct of the three. "Lord," I thought, "that is certainly the truth. I need a lot more discretion."

As the next step in this revealing process, the Lord began to take me through a little review of my spiritual walk. He reminded me of the many times I had made mistakes, not through lack of understanding or insight but through lack of discretion.

Proverbs 2:8 says that God *"guards the paths of justice, and preserves the way of His saints."* Verse 11 says, *"Discretion will preserve you; understanding will keep you."* In other words, understanding, insight, and discretion stand over us for our protection. They are like the Lord's secret service agents, on guard to watch over us and see that nothing harms us.

In the next chapter, we will see how these three attributes help us to better know the Lord.

7

FOUR CONDITIONS FOR KNOWING GOD

Having looked at three aspects of wisdom—understanding, insight, and discretion—let's go back and reread Proverbs 2:1–5:

> *My son, if you receive my words, and treasure my commands within you, so that you incline your ear to wisdom, and apply your heart to understanding; yes, if you cry out for discernment, and lift up your voice for understanding, if you seek her as silver, and search for her as for hidden treasures; then you will understand the fear of the* Lord, *and find the knowledge of God.* (Proverbs 2:1–5)

MEETING THE CONDITIONS

Analyzing the construction of the verses above, we recognize four conditions we must meet in order to obtain the goal of knowing God.

These promises, like most of the promises in the Bible, are conditional. In other words, God says, "If you will do this, then I will do that." For example, we saw in chapter 2 that God promised to be Israel's Doctor—"*if you diligently heed the voice of the* Lord *your God*" (Exodus 15:26). If the Israelites ignored that condition of heeding His voice, they had no right to claim the Lord as their Doctor.

Typical of Hebrew poetry, each of these conditions is stated in a couplet—two parallel statements that together make up the whole statement. To get the full meaning, we must put both statements together. The ultimate goal is specified in the final verse: "*Then you will understand the fear of the* Lord, *and find the knowledge of God*" (Proverbs 2:5).

This goal is so vital that it can scarcely be put into words. It is the very heart of this entire book: finding the knowledge of God. Once again, this is what Israel missed—and what you and I *don't* want to miss.

We noted in an earlier chapter that Israel bypassed the primary purpose of redemption that God expressed in Exodus 19:4: "*I bore you on eagles' wings and brought you to Myself.*" We observed that Israel received the law, embraced the covenant, and entered the promised land. Even so, most of them never found the knowledge of God. Sadly, they overlooked His primary purpose for them. It was not to bring them to the law, or to the covenant, or to entrance into the land. His aim was to bring them to the knowledge of Himself.

Not only do the first four verses of Proverbs 2 show us our need for the knowledge of God, but they also show us the pathway to obtain it. I am a practically minded person in spiritual things, so I want to be able to say, "The knowledge of God is what we need—and *here is the pathway* to attain it." The pathway is presented in four "if" statements before the goal is revealed. Let's consider these four conditions before discussing the goal more fully in chapter 8.

1. RECEIVE GOD'S WORDS

The first condition we must meet in order to know God is to be receptive to His words: *"If you receive my words, and treasure my commands within you…"* (Proverbs 2:1). The apostle James urges his readers to *"lay aside all filthiness and overflow of wickedness, and receive with meekness the implanted word, which is able to save your souls"* (James 1:21). Many people listen to the Word of God but never truly receive it. Why? Because receiving often requires meekness. We cannot merely listen to God's Word and let it pass us by; we must be receptive to it and be willing to submit to its authority. This is the first requirement.

God's primary means of revelation is His written Word. If we bypass His Word, we have no right to expect revelation from Him. If we receive the Word, revelation will come through it, and then through other ways as well. Anyone who does not receive the Word cannot expect to receive revelation by some other channel. (Actually, if they do receive such revelation from another source, it will likely be deception.) We must begin, therefore, by receiving God's Word and treasuring or storing up His commands, keeping them in a sure, secure place within us.

How do you react to God's commands? Do you resent them? Or do you treasure them? Many people in today's culture are often suspicious of authority, and they are likely to reject anyone who tells them what to do. There is a spirit abroad in the earth today claiming that "anyone who tries to tell me what to do is the enemy." But God says, "I want you to receive and treasure My commands." His commandments are given for our good—not to make life difficult but to preserve us and make us successful. For each of us, it is not sufficient merely to hear God's words of instruction. We must treasure them within us.

One familiar but important practice I highly recommend is memorizing Scripture. This is a simple way we can treasure God's commands within us. People often tell me, "I can't memorize Scripture. My mind simply doesn't retain it." But the same person will go to the doctor, have a fifteen-minute consultation, and then come out and repeat verbatim nearly everything the doctor said. Generally, we remember what we consider to be important.

2. INCLINE YOUR EAR

The second condition we must meet is as follows: *"If you incline your ear to wisdom and direct your heart to understanding..."* (Proverbs 2:2 BSB).

The inclined ear is one of the repeated themes of Proverbs. To *incline* means "to bow down." You cannot bow down your ear without bowing down your head. What does the inclined head represent? *Humility* or *teachability.*

I mentioned in chapter 2 that when I was hospitalized during World War II and the doctors were unable to heal me, I realized that if I were to get out of the hospital, it would have to be God's doing. So, I began to study the theme of healing in the Bible. Throughout its pages, I found repeated promises about healing, long life, strength, and prosperity.

All of these truths seemed in stark contrast to my religious upbringing in the Anglican Church. My religious background consisted of twenty years of churchgoing, believing that being a Christian meant being miserable. For me, that price was too high for what little benefit I saw in the Christian faith that I deemed desirable. So, here I was, as a new believer, coming face-to-face with these unfamiliar truths in the Bible. It was hard for me to believe God truly wanted me to prosper, to be successful, and to be healthy. Every time I came across such a clear statement in Scripture, I said to myself, "It can't be that way. This can't be true."

Finally, one day, as I was reasoning like this, the Lord spoke to my spirit and said, *Now, tell Me: who is the Teacher and who is the pupil?*

I replied, "Lord, You are the Teacher, and I am the pupil."

He said, *Well, then, would you mind letting Me teach you?*

Immediately, I saw that I had not "inclined my ear." I had been unwilling to hear what God was saying. Again, the lesson I learned that day as I lay in my hospital bed was this truth: more than anything else, healing depends on listening to God.

With my ear now inclined, the passage that ultimately freed me from the hospital and brought me through to complete healing was Proverbs 4:20–22:

> *My son, give attention to my words; incline your ear to my sayings. Do not let them depart from your eyes; keep them in the midst of your heart; for they are life to those who find them, and health to all their flesh.*

To me, this was as comprehensive a promise of health as you can find anywhere in the Bible. But its fulfillment depends entirely upon our attitude toward God's Word.

Many people find it difficult to incline their ear. By nature, we humans are stubborn, proud, and unteachable. We have formed our own concepts of what Christianity should be and what the Bible has to say to us. Generally, people's ears are not inclined to hear what God says. How desperately we need to take the action described in the second requirement: *"If you incline your ear to wisdom and direct your heart to understanding..."* (Proverbs 2:2 BSB).

Just as an added commentary, the command to *"direct your heart"* brings up another key word in Proverbs: *diligence*. To direct your heart is to be diligent in seeking to understand and take in all that God wants to say to you.

Diligent application requires time. You and I cannot apply our hearts to anything without giving time to it. Few Christians give sufficient time to the Bible, which is one of the church's root problems. If believers would exchange the amount of time they spend watching television or using their mobile devices for the amount of time they spend with their Bibles, they would be amazed at how spiritually minded they would become. Social media and television, even Christian programs, tend to make people more and more passive. People become accustomed to flipping channels or staring at their digital devices, simply letting things pass in front of their eyes. In contrast to those practices, "directing your heart" takes effort.

One modern philosophy in education today insists that learning should be fun. The belief is that if it is too difficult or involves hard work, it must be wrong. But attaining knowledge and applying discipline *are* hard work. These and many other aspects of maturity in the natural and spiritual realms will never be achieved without hard work. If we are not prepared to work hard, we will never reach our God-given potential. Once again, it is disappointing to observe those who spend most of their time on secondary pursuits rather than setting their sights on primary things that will matter for eternity.

Here is my challenge to all of us from Proverbs 2:2: "*Incline your ear to wisdom and direct your heart to understanding*" (BSB).

3. CRY OUT TO GOD

The third requirement for attaining the knowledge of God is stated in Proverbs 2:3: "*If you cry out for discernment, and lift up your voice for understanding....*"

Notice how *discernment* and *understanding* come to us: by our crying out and lifting up our voices. These actions signify fervent prayer—more than just the tepid prayer of the average church member: "God, bless me and my wife, my son and his wife; us four, no more." That is not crying out!

I cannot explain all of God's dealings, but I know there are times when He looks for us to be desperate. God values desperation in us, and sometimes He waits until we cry out and lift up our voices. The Scriptures say that Jesus Himself prayed "*with vehement cries and tears*" (Hebrews 5:7). In His sufferings, He gave Himself totally in prayer.

When we experience difficulty, we may ask, "God, why are You letting all this happen to me?" I believe there are times when God would answer, *I'm waiting for you to be desperate.*

We may reply, "Lord, why do You want me desperate?" When I have asked that question, this is how God has responded: *Because that's the only way you can express your appreciation for what I am offering you. Until you are prepared to be desperate, you won't appreciate what I'm offering.*

For instance, I have come to understand two truths regarding ministering to seekers: that the baptism in the Holy Spirit is for the thirsty and that deliverance from evil spirits is for the desperate. Some people wonder why they are not delivered. Often, the answer is that they are not desperate. I have told some people who were seeking deliverance, "God doesn't deliver you from your 'friends.' You're not desperate enough. Come back when you are." It is surprising how desperate that advice makes them!

Over the years, I have refrained from arguing with people over theological issues about the baptism in the Holy Spirit. The baptism is not for the theologically correct. Jesus said, *"If anyone thirsts, let him come to Me and drink"* (John 7:37). Bypass the argumentative and go to the thirsty. Bypass the argumentative and go for the desperate. That is the way God does it.

The third condition for knowing God, then, suggests the element of fervent prayer.

4. BE SINGLE-MINDED

The fourth condition we must meet in order to obtain the goal of knowing God is found in Proverbs 2:4: *"If you seek her as silver, and search for her as for hidden treasures...."*

This verse reminds me of Jesus's parable of the treasure hidden in the field. (See Matthew 13:44.) Do you remember what the man had to do to obtain the treasure? He had to buy the field. I have often pictured that man looking at his recent purchase—a big, useless-looking plot of ground, overgrown with thistles, having no apparent commercial value. All around him, people are saying, "Why did that man make such a foolish investment?" On the surface, it was all true. But there was something in that field nobody else knew about. The man had found a wonderful treasure, and he knew he could not get his hands on it until he bought the field. He had no legal right to take the treasure until he owned that field. So, he sold all he had, paid the price for the field, and then started to dig for the treasure.

Digging is hard work. It brings blisters and sore muscles. I believe the Lord is telling us through Proverbs 2:4 that hard work is the price we pay for wisdom.

This final condition encompasses the three previous requirements—receiving God's words, inclining your ear, and crying out to God. They all involve single-mindedness of attitude. Anyone who fulfills the first three conditions is already single-minded. They have identified what they are seeking, and they are determined to get it.

Single-mindedness is an essential element of success in any area of life. In contrast, the Bible says, *"a double-minded man* [is] *unstable in all his ways"* (James 1:8). James says God will not answer the prayers of a double-minded person. (See verse 7.)

You've probably heard the common expression "If you aim for nothing, you can be sure you'll hit it!" There are few conditions more tragic than being aimless and unmotivated in life. Dear reader, don't allow yourself to fall into that trap. You can make mistakes as a child of God, and God will overlook them and even use them. But do not become aimless and unmotivated, because that insults the Lord.

Let's be frank with ourselves: how many unprofitable hours do we spend in useless activity? Paul says, *"He who sows to his flesh will of the flesh reap corruption"* (Galatians 6:8). Spending hours upon hours on wasteful activities is sowing to the flesh. Please bear in mind that when we spend our time unwisely, we are sowing to our flesh. The result is that we will reap what we have sown.

Instead, let's set our aim to be single-minded in pursuing a close relationship with the Lord. If we do, we will reach the goal that will be covered in the next chapter.

8

THE GOAL OF SEEKING

We now come to the conclusion and goal of the four "if" verses: *"Then you will understand the fear of the LORD, and find the knowledge of God"* (Proverbs 2:5).

I explained earlier that, in Hebrew poetry, the two halves of a verse complement one another. To get the full meaning, we must combine those two halves. In this case, I believe these two aspects of the promise go together. Solomon is telling us that we cannot find the knowledge of God without the fear of the Lord—without having a deep sense of awe and reverence toward the One who created us, loves us, and saved us. The fear of the Lord is the essential condition for—and has an indispensable role in—our coming to know God. God does not reveal Himself to those who do not fear Him. When we fear Him, we will diligently seek Him; we will align ourselves with His purposes and ways. Then we will *"find the knowledge of God."*

A PICTURE OF THE FEAR OF THE LORD

Before we consider a number of Scriptures about the fear of the Lord—since this is a primary theme of the Bible—please allow me to give you a mental image that may convey a deeper comprehension of the meaning of this phrase.

Imagine that you are standing on a very high mountain. It is a place of incredible grandeur and beauty. From this elevated place, you can look up into the heavens and see the glory of the skies. In the same manner, you can gaze down at the earth and see the splendor of the sea, the mountains, the fields, and the forests. The delightful views are inexhaustible. However, immediately in front of you is a steep cliff plunging down hundreds of feet, just beyond a railing that protects you from falling over. If you lean toward that railing, fear clutches you in the pit of your stomach, and you say to yourself, "If I were to lean a little farther, I would topple down this mountain to my destruction."

That is how I picture the fear of the Lord. You can go so far—but the consequences of a misstep are perilous. It is tremendously important that we allow the Holy Spirit to impart the fear of the Lord to us. Let's look further at what Scripture has to say about this topic.

THE DELIGHT OF THE MESSIAH

The book of Revelation presents the Holy Spirit as *"seven lamps of fire…burning before the throne"* (Revelation 4:5) of God. These lamps are referred to as *"the seven Spirits of God"* (verse 5) or *"the sevenfold Spirit of God"* (verse 5 NLT). I have always taught that the sevenfold Spirit of God is represented in the first few verses of Isaiah 11—verses that present a prophetic picture of Jesus as the Messiah:

> *There shall come forth a Rod from the stem of Jesse, and a Branch shall grow out of his roots. The Spirit of the LORD shall rest upon Him, the Spirit of wisdom and understanding, the Spirit of counsel and might, the Spirit of knowledge and of the fear of the LORD.* (Isaiah 11:1–2)

First, Isaiah 11:2 specifies *"the Spirit of the LORD"*—referring to how the Spirit speaks in the first person as God. For example, Acts 13:2 states, *"The Holy Spirit said, 'Now separate to Me Barnabas and Saul for the work to which I have called them.'"* The Holy Spirit was speaking as the Lord to the church leaders.

The passage from Isaiah continues, *"The Spirit of wisdom and understanding."* These are the second and third notable qualities of God's Spirit. Then we have *"the Spirit of counsel and might"* as the fourth and fifth qualities. Finally, *"the Spirit of knowledge and of the fear of the LORD"* are listed as the sixth and seventh attributes.

Please notice that, as in Proverbs 2:5, knowledge and the fear of the Lord are united. I stated earlier that it is dangerous to have knowledge without the fear of the Lord because *"knowledge puffs up"* (1 Corinthians 8:1), while the fear of the Lord keeps us humble and safe.

Let's keep in mind that Isaiah 11:1–2 is a prophetic picture of the Messiah and of the sevenfold aspects of the Spirit that rest upon Him, and that one of those aspects is *"the Spirit of...the fear of the LORD."* It is a good reminder that if Jesus, the Messiah, needed the fear of the Lord, which one of us can say that we do not?

The very next verse, Isaiah 11:3, emphasizes this attribute of the Messiah:

> *His delight is in the fear of the* Lord, *and He shall not judge by the sight of His eyes, nor decide by the hearing of His ears.*

The one aspect singled out and mentioned above all others in the Isaiah 11 prophecy about the Messiah is the fear of the Lord. Jesus *delighted* in the fear of the Lord. Can we do less?

Let's also consider Psalm 19:9:

> *The fear of the* Lord *is clean, enduring forever.*

If there is one factor that will keep you spiritually clean, it is the fear of the Lord. Furthermore, the fear of the Lord will never come to an end.

In 2 Corinthians 7:1, Paul says, "*Let us cleanse ourselves from all filthiness of the flesh and spirit, perfecting holiness in the fear of God.*" The surest protection against filthiness of flesh and spirit is the fear of the Lord.

GOD TEACHES THOSE WHO FEAR HIM

If you and I meditate on the following Scriptures about the fear of the Lord and allow them to penetrate our hearts, the impact will be significant.

> *Behold, the fear of the Lord, that is wisdom, and to depart from evil is understanding.* (Job 28:28)

Without the fear of the Lord, there is no true wisdom. Why? Because the fear of God always causes you to depart from evil. The fear of the Lord and delighting in evil are mutually exclusive.

Who is the man that fears the Lord*? Him shall He teach in the way He chooses.* (Psalm 25:12)

God teaches the one who fears Him. He chooses His students not by intellectual qualifications but by character. How wise He is! Many institutions choose their students by intellectual qualifications—and they often make some very unwise choices. God is not so foolish. The psalmist writes this about the person who fears the Lord:

He himself ["his soul" KJV, NASB, BSB*] shall dwell in prosperity, and his descendants shall inherit the earth. The secret of the* Lord *is with those who fear Him, and He will show them His covenant.* (Psalm 25:13–14)

Knowledge of God's covenant comes by revelation, and God reveals His covenant to those who fear Him. If you do not receive the knowledge of God and His covenant by revelation, you cannot receive it. And unless the Holy Spirit has prepared your heart, you will never truly grasp it.

Letting God show you His covenant will give you an understanding of Him and a sense of security that you can know in no other manner. As we have previously discussed, there is no way to find true security except by knowing God personally. Ultimate security must be rooted in a personal knowledge of the Lord.

A major handicap I have seen among my fellow Christian leaders is personal insecurity. It causes them to attempt to achieve security apart from knowing God and being led by the Spirit. Insecurity and rejection, moreover, are two of the major problems of contemporary society—and the solution to both is found in God. When you and I know in our hearts that God has accepted us, we need not be troubled with human rejection ever again.

> *Come, you children, listen to me; I will teach you the fear of the* LORD*. Who is the man who desires life, and loves many days, that he may see good?* (Psalm 34:11–12)

Please notice again that the fear of the Lord must be taught. Christian leaders can help in the process, but ultimately, we will learn it from God Himself.

CHOOSING THE FEAR OF THE LORD

In Proverbs 1:28–29, God speaks as the personification of wisdom:

> *Then they will call on me, but I will not answer; they will seek me diligently, but they will not find me. Because they hated knowledge and did not choose the fear of the* LORD*....*

Once more, the writer of Proverbs is linking knowledge and the fear of the Lord. Please notice especially that the fear of the Lord must be *chosen*. The people whom God did not answer had not chosen the fear of the Lord. The result of their failure was the judgment of God. The Lord withdraws Himself from those who reject His provision.

Let's pause for a moment and each ask ourselves, "Have I chosen the fear of the Lord?" If we have not, we are in danger of finding ourselves in the category of people mentioned in this passage and of tragically missing our opportunity to know Him. That should be a sobering thought!

The following are some additional verses about the fear of the Lord:

The fear of the Lord is the beginning of wisdom.
(Psalm 111:10)

Beginning means "the primary part." In other words, true wisdom is impossible without the fear of the Lord.

The fear of the Lord is the beginning of wisdom, and the knowledge of the Holy One is understanding.
(Proverbs 9:10)

Yet again, the fear of the Lord, wisdom, and knowledge are linked.

The fear of the Lord is the beginning of knowledge.
(Proverbs 1:7)

Not only is the fear of the Lord the beginning of wisdom, but it is also the beginning of knowledge. The writer is talking not about intellectual acuity but spiritual knowledge—especially the knowledge of God Himself.

THE GREATEST BENEFITS

I know of no single pursuit for which greater benefits are promised in Scripture than the fear of the Lord. Once you are introduced to these promises, you will want to pursue them for yourself. They are truly staggering!

The fear of the Lord prolongs days, but the years of the wicked will be shortened. (Proverbs 10:27)

Long life is a recurrent theme connected with the fear of the Lord. (We just saw this clearly in Psalm 34:11–12.) If you desire long life, choose the fear of the Lord.

> *In the fear of the* Lord *there is strong confidence, and His children will have a place of refuge. The fear of the* Lord *is a fountain of life, to turn one away from the snares of death.* (Proverbs 14:26–27)

"Strong confidence" is the opposite of insecurity; it provides a place of refuge. Please note that an additional benefit—a second main theme associated here with the fear of the Lord—is *"life."*

> *The fear of the* Lord *leads to life, and he who has it will abide in satisfaction; he will not be visited with evil.* (Proverbs 19:23)

This verse presents one of the most astonishing promises in all of Scripture. What more could you ask for than what is promised here? To *"abide in satisfaction"* could also be translated to "abide satisfied." Life, satisfaction, and exemption from evil are all benefits of the fear of the Lord. The corollary to this promise is that dissatisfied people do not fear the Lord. If you meet a dissatisfied, discontented person, you can be sure that they do not fear the Lord.

> *By humility and the fear of the* Lord *are riches and honor and life.* (Proverbs 22:4)

This promise should cause us to praise God in a grateful way. Personally, I would be depriving God of His glory if I did not testify that all of this has been proven in my own experience. I remember well the times when I was not prospering. There were occasions back then when I had to buy my razor blades one at a time because I could not afford a pack of them. But I have seen God's faithfulness. As I have continued to live in obedience and the fear of the Lord to the best of my ability, He has prospered me. (I say all this with the sober reminder that if any of us puts riches and honor ahead of fearing the Lord, we will go astray.)

As we conclude this chapter, we arrive at the greatest benefit of the fear of the Lord. That benefit brings us back to the main theme of this book. Once we have met each of the four conditions in Proverbs 2:1–4—receive God's words, incline your ear, cry out to God, and be single-minded—and once we are living in the fear of the Lord, we will experience the promise at the end of verse 5:

Then you will...find the knowledge of God.

9

INTO GOD'S PRESENCE

The tabernacle of Moses is one of my favorite biblical illustrations of how to come into the knowledge of God. And nothing in Scripture gives me a greater desire for personal holiness than studying the tabernacle. It makes holiness alive and real to me. Let me simply say that this subject has never failed to excite me, and I hope I can convey some of that excitement to you as well. So then, as we explore the blessings of attaining the knowledge of God, let us consider the tabernacle as a picture of the way into a close relationship with Him.

THE PATTERN OF THE TABERNACLE

This extraordinary structure of the tabernacle is described at length in the book of Exodus, as well as in the epistle to the Hebrews. It was erected in the wilderness of Sinai more than three thousand years ago, configured according to the heavenly pattern God gave Moses. (See, for example, Hebrews 8:5.) The tabernacle was built to be movable. God did not simply sanctify a piece of real estate somewhere. As God led His people in the wilderness, wherever the tabernacle was erected and the conditions were met, that place became sanctified.

The tabernacle had three main sections: the outer court, the Holy Place behind the first veil or curtain, and the Holy of Holies behind the second veil or curtain. The outermost wall of the tabernacle was a linen fence surrounding a courtyard that was approximately 150 feet long and 75 feet wide. The fence itself was about seven and a half feet high. Inside the courtyard was a large altar, a laver (or basin) of bronze, and the tent itself. The entire courtyard was open to the sky and the elements.

The tent stood at one end of the courtyard opposite the entrance, and it was covered with badger skins—outwardly, not impressive or particularly beautiful. Inside the tent were the two sections described above: the Holy Place and the Holy of Holies.

We begin in the outer court—in the physical, natural realm. In the outer court, the main object was the bronze altar of sacrifice on which all the sacrificial animals were killed and offered to God. This bronze altar typifies for us Christ's sacrificial death on our behalf. It speaks of the blood that He shed so that we might be redeemed and reconciled to God. And that's the starting point. We cannot bypass the cross for reconciling with God and following the path to knowing Him.

There are different ways in which we might view the meaning of the first and second veils of the tabernacle. For instance, in Hebrews 10:19–20, the author compares the second veil to the body of Jesus—both having been "torn" at Christ's death on the cross. (See Matthew 27:51; Mark 15:38.)

As I have studied the tabernacle as a picture of our coming into the knowledge of God, I have come to see the veils in a further way. The first veil, I believe, may typify Christ's resurrection. When we pass through that veil, we pass into an area that has been opened to us by the resurrection of Jesus from the dead. It signifies, in a sense, our identification with Christ not only in His death and burial but also in His resurrection. The Scripture says that we died with Him, but we have also been raised with Him. For example, Paul tells us in Ephesians 2:5–6:

> *Even when we were dead in trespasses,* [God] *made us alive together with Christ (by grace you have been saved), and raised us up together, and made us sit together in the heavenly places in Christ Jesus.*

Please notice that all that is spoken in this verse is in the past tense. It has been accomplished! Don't settle for any destination lower than the throne because that is where you belong! The "throne life" is represented by the Holy of Holies, the place behind the second veil.

The second veil may typify ascension that takes us into the heavenlies and seats us on the throne with Christ. Jesus ascended to the right hand of God as our "*forerunner*" (Hebrews 6:20) and has prepared the way for us to follow Him. We gain access to the Holy of Holies not just through Jesus's death and resurrection but also by His ascension.

In the Holy of Holies, in the presence of God, are two key activities that I mentioned in an earlier chapter. These pursuits are valuable in themselves: *fellowship* and *worship*. In the Holy of Holies, we truly enter into these activities. Fellowship is typified by the two golden cherubim that face one another over the ark of the covenant, their wings stretched out, meeting over the center.

This is a beautiful picture of fellowship. And our response is worship.

Worship in the Spirit is, in the truest sense, the union of our spirit with God's. In that regard, Paul says something very strange in 1 Corinthians 6:16–17: *"He who is joined to a harlot is one body with her.... But he who is joined to the Lord is one spirit with Him."* You cannot separate the two sections of that statement. There is a physical union of sex that makes two persons one flesh. But there is a spiritual union with God that makes us *"one spirit with Him."* Can you see how far this goes beyond our being merely "religious" or attending church? Worship is the union of our spirit with God's. We come to know God when we recognize we are enthroned with Jesus Christ, our Great High Priest. With that being a reality, we have become *"a chosen generation, a royal priesthood, a holy nation, His own special people"* (1 Peter 2:9). We will explore these truths further in coming chapters.

DIFFERENT TYPES OF LIGHT

We can better understand the three sections of the tabernacle—the courtyard, the Holy Place, and the Holy of Holies—by noting the type of light available to each. In the outer courtyard, the light was natural—the sun by day, the moon and stars by night. The outer courtyard symbolizes our natural understanding. Then, moving through the first curtain into the Holy Place, there was no more natural light. The light in that narrow space, which was about thirty feet long and fifteen feet wide, was artificial. It was provided by a lampstand holding seven lamps, each filled with pure olive oil. Thus, beyond the first curtain, all movement was by faith and not by sight, since the first curtain shut off all natural light.

Finally, behind the second curtain, the Holy of Holies was the most sacred place on earth at that time. In that tiny section, a cube about fifteen feet wide, fifteen feet deep, and fifteen feet high—which to me signifies the triune God—there was only one piece of furniture. Again, this was the resting place of the ark of the covenant, with the cherubim overhanging it. In the Holy of Holies, there was no natural light and no artificial light. The only light was supplied by the supernatural presence of almighty God indwelling that small area within that tent and the ark as the symbol of His presence. This was the place where God would meet with Moses to give him instructions for the people to follow, and it was the place where the high priest would enter once a year on the Day of Atonement as the representative of God's people. (See, for example, Exodus 25:22; Hebrews 9:7.)

The light associated with these three sections of the tabernacle has parallels with discovering the knowledge of God. To find it, we must step from the courtyard with its natural light (the realm of natural knowledge and understanding) and move beyond the Holy Place, lit by the artificial light of the seven-branched lampstand (representing spiritual revelation—the Word of God illuminated by the Holy Spirit—which does not depend on natural knowledge) and into the Holy of Holies (having no natural or artificial light of any kind, representing the realm of relationship). Revelation in the Holy of Holies (God's presence) does not come by natural revelation or even faith through the Word of God but by personal encounter.

Please use this illustration to consider what is involved in our desire to discover the knowledge of God. To the natural mind, the process seems crazy. First, we must leave the sun, moon, and stars to step inside a narrow space where light is provided by the seven-branched lampstand. Once more, this lampstand, filled with pure olive oil, represents the Holy Spirit's illumination of God's Word.

But for those of us who want the knowledge of God, we can't stop there. Our ultimate destination is the Holy of Holies, beyond the inner curtain where it is totally dark. Dark, that is, unless the supernatural presence of God fills it with what in Hebrew is called the *shekinah,* which means "dwelling" or "resting." Why would we want to go there? There is only one reason: to meet with God.

Ultimately, a desire to meet with God is the motivation that leads to the knowledge of God. In the Holy of Holies, you are not even dependent on Scripture. Our faith and practice must never supersede Scripture; it is always the ultimate authority, and no "revelation" that departs from Scripture is from God. But in the Holy of Holies, you come into a direct revelation of God Himself.

ADDITIONAL SYMBOLS OF THE TABERNACLE

Let us now look at two additional ways in which the components of the tabernacle are symbolic for our walk of faith. The fivefold ministry gifts of Ephesians 4:11—apostle, prophet, evangelist, pastor, and teacher—represent the area within the first compartment, the Holy Place. But two further ministries God has destined for us are the highest, and they are symbolized in the second compartment, the Holy of Holies. These ministries are those of *priest* and *king,* the two ultimate ministries of Jesus. He fulfills these ministries for all eternity as High Priest after the order of Melchizedek, sitting at God's right hand. (See Hebrews 7:1–17; 10:12.)

I would also suggest that the three areas of the tabernacle—the outer courtyard, the Holy Place, and the Holy of Holies—represent the three areas of every human being: the body, the soul, and the spirit. Through its natural senses, the body discerns the revelation of God's existence and attributes as demonstrated through the created world. (See Romans 1:20.) The soul knows *about* God with the kind of knowledge that comes from Bible teaching and theology, illuminated by the Holy Spirit. But the spirit knows God Himself.

A LIVING RELATIONSHIP

Let's respond to what we have learned so far. The tabernacle is a symbolic way to represent finding the knowledge of God. This discovery is difficult to express in theological terms, because the human mind cannot formulate a theology that will encompass all of who God is. That is why God, in His infinite wisdom, has chosen such pictures as the tabernacle to describe the way to the knowledge of Himself. A knowledge of God cannot be attained through study or religious exercises. It comes only as we follow our God-given desire to know Him personally and intimately, refusing to settle for anything less. As emphasized repeatedly, knowing God in a personal relationship is the ultimate reason for our redemption. It is our ultimate destination as a child of God.

My deepest hope is that I have inspired you through this teaching to go beyond the second veil into a living relationship with God Himself. I invite you to proclaim out loud the verses we examined earlier, Proverbs 2:1–5. As you proclaim them, meditate on the meaning of each phrase, affirming in your heart all that it means to you.

> *My son, if you receive my words, and treasure my commands within you, so that you incline your ear to wisdom, and apply your heart to understanding; yes, if you cry out for discernment, and lift up your voice for understanding, if you seek her as silver, and search for her as for hidden treasures; then you will understand the fear of the* Lord, *and find the knowledge of God.*

Thus, as you think about your life, consider where you stand in relation to the tabernacle of Moses. Are you in the outer court, where you live only by what you can see and experience with your natural senses, natural reason, and natural emotions? Are you situated in the Holy Place, where you live by faith in the light of God's Word as it is illuminated by the Holy Spirit? This is a wonderful and blessed place to be, and it is worthy of commendation for the faithfulness required to be there. Or are you also stepping daily behind the veil into the Holy of Holies, into the very presence of God Himself?

If your heart's desire is to know God in all His fullness, are you willing to choose the fear of the Lord and delight yourself in it? This may still sound like an unusual invitation, but I am confident that if you are willing, God Himself will teach you to live in this way.

If you choose to walk in the fear of the Lord so you may enter behind the veil into the Holy of Holies, please declare the following proclamation out loud as we conclude this chapter:

> I choose the fear of the Lord!
>
> Father God, I choose the fear of the Lord. Teach me the fear of the Lord so that I may find the knowledge of You within the Holy of Holies. In Jesus's name, amen.

PART TWO:

FULFILLING OUR DESTINY

"There is a calling for every saved person—
a unique way of life, a unique task,
a unique responsibility."
—Derek Prince

10

OUR PURPOSE IN LIFE

We have seen that God's purpose in redeeming His people Israel, when He brought them out of slavery and made His covenant with them at Mount Sinai, was to bring them to Himself. But the redeemed people of God have often overlooked this purpose and reached for the benefits while bypassing a true relationship with God Himself. Most of the problems experienced by God's redeemed people can be traced to this one cause. We have neglected the knowledge of God and pursued only the benefits He gives. Yet as important and wonderful as these benefits may be, they are secondary to knowing God Himself.

We have also noted the two unvarying requirements God sets in all His dealings with His redeemed people: first, *that we listen to His voice* (or "listen listening"), and, second, *that we keep His covenant*. The goal of our lives should be a personal relationship with God in which we hear His voice. Biblical faith is not primarily an intellectual conviction but a personal commitment of loyalty—first and foremost to God, then to His redeemed people.

Covenantal relationship can be typified by the two beams of the cross, the vertical and the horizontal. The vertical beam represents our relationship with God, and the horizontal represents our relationships with God's redeemed people. If one beam is out of line, the other will be also. If our relationships with one another are out of line, then our relationship with God is out of line. If our relationship with God is right, our relationships with our fellow believers will be right also.

This brief synopsis brings us to the overall purpose of knowing God personally: that we might become His own special people, a kingdom of priests, and a holy nation.

GOD'S PURPOSE FOR HIS PEOPLE

Once again, God's purpose for His people, told originally to Israel in Exodus 19:4–6, is restated (in a slightly different order) for all believers in 1 Peter 2:9:

> *You are a chosen generation, a royal priesthood, a holy nation, His own special people.*

Let's examine the various aspects of this purpose more closely.

A CHOSEN GENERATION

First, we are *"a chosen generation."* Let me be very clear: we must acknowledge that everything proceeds ultimately from God's choice, not man's choice. A great error can creep into our thinking if we believe that everything about our destiny happens because we made a decision. Oh, no! It all happens because

God decided. Jesus said to His disciples, "*You did not choose Me, but I chose you*" (John 15:16). I do not believe this refers to the choice of salvation but rather to that of apostleship. The emphasis here is on the Lord's choice.

James writes about all those who are born again, "*Of His own will* [God] *brought us forth by the word of truth*" (James 1:18). Redemption did not start with the will of humanity. It started with the will of God. Ephesians reveals that God's choice was made in eternity. If you and I can grasp the fact that God "*chose us in* [Christ] *before the foundation of the world*" (Ephesians 1:4), we will be able to rest securely in that truth. When we do, many of our tensions and anxieties will fade away.

In 2 Timothy 1:9, Paul makes this statement about the Lord:

> [He] *has saved us and called us with a holy calling, not according to our works, but according to His own purpose and grace which was given to us in Christ Jesus before time began.*

Isn't this an astonishing statement? Please bear in mind that when God saves you, He also calls you. There is a calling for every saved person—a unique way of life, a unique task, a unique responsibility. Because you and I are saved, God has a calling for us. If we have not yet discovered it, we truly have not yet found the purpose of our life. His calling was given to us out of His grace "*before time began.*"

It is a staggering thought that nothing happens as an accident of time. Everything about our destiny proceeds out of the eternal mind and counsel of God. It all depends on His choice. At a certain point, we must say "yes" to God's choice. But if God had never made the choice, we would have nothing to respond to.

A ROYAL PRIESTHOOD AND A HOLY NATION

Two other aspects of God's purpose in redeeming His people, based on 1 Peter 2:9, are to make us *"a royal priesthood and a holy nation."* The word *royal* refers to a king or queen. Whether this term is translated *"a royal priesthood"* or, as in Exodus 19:6, *"a kingdom of priests,"* it is the same thought. We are to be a kingdom of priests and a holy nation. We will look at this truth in more detail in the chapters ahead.

The church of Jesus Christ is a nation—not in the manner of Great Britain, China, or Poland, but a new nation under the lordship of Jesus Christ, brought into being by its citizens' rebirth through faith in Jesus Christ. The church is a holy nation, therefore, set apart to God for His purposes.

HIS OWN SPECIAL PEOPLE

A further purpose of God in redeeming us is to make us *"His own special people."* The Creator of the universe has selected us! Isn't it a mind-boggling thought that we are God's own special possession in the earth?

I have often asked myself, "What is God seeking out of human history?" I believe the answer is found in Deuteronomy 32:9: *"The LORD's portion is His people."* Out of anything in all history that the Lord could select, what is His goal? God desires a people for Himself, and everything He does centers around His people. If you and I can see all of this in the right perspective, we will be able to see ourselves in the right perspective. We are God's desire and choice.

Paul writes to the Corinthian church, *"All things are for your sakes"* (2 Corinthians 4:15). Even though the Corinthians were not the most spiritual Christians, Paul is saying that everything that happens to them—and to us as believers—happens with reference to us as sons and daughters of God. The sun rises and sets for you and me. The tides ebb and flow for you and me. Everything good and edifying in this world is for our sakes.

"All things are for [our] *sakes."* Why? Because we are God's own special people, His special treasures. We are the chosen receptacle in the universe upon which He has bestowed His greatest creative ability.

GOD'S CREATIVE ABILITY

In this regard—the display of God's limitless creativity—let us consider these words from Ephesians 2:10:

> *We are His workmanship, created in Christ Jesus for good works, which God prepared beforehand that we should walk in them.*

This truth is similar to what we see in 1 Peter 2:9. When the Word says, *"We are His workmanship,"* the Greek word translated as *"workmanship"* is *poiema*. From this root, we get the English word *poem*. We are not an afterthought; we are God's creative masterpiece!

This thought blesses me every time I meditate on it. When God wanted to bring forth His masterpiece to dazzle the entire universe, He did so by using fallen humanity for His material. The Creator decided to use us to demonstrate the limitless capacity of His creative ability.

Let's keep in mind, then, that you and I were not created to please ourselves or to live in whatever way we wish. Ephesians 2:10 says that we were *"created in Christ Jesus for good works, which God prepared beforehand that we should walk in them."* Paul reiterated this truth in 2 Timothy 1:9, which we read earlier:

> [God] *has saved us and called us with a holy calling, not according to our works, but according to His own purpose and grace which was given to us in Christ Jesus before time began.*

The decision is not ours regarding what we are going to do as Christians. It is not a matter of making up our minds about our plans for our lives. Rather, our task is to find out what God has chosen for us to do. He has good works, prepared before time began, for every person who is His redeemed. We will experience our ultimate fulfillment when we discover what those good works are and walk in them. Paul reminds us that these are *"not according to our works"* based on our own natural ability. Rather, they proceed from God's supernatural grace.

Over the years, I have observed that God often chooses the most improbable people to perform works for Him. By way of example, I was the only child in my family, with no brothers or sisters. To me, girls were mysterious entities I did not understand—and I was content to leave unexplained and unexplored! In the purposes of God, however, in 1946, I married a Danish lady, Lydia, who had a very different cultural background from my own. On the day I married her, I not only became her husband, but I also became the father of her eight adopted daughters. That made me the only male in a household of nine women. Believe me, the adjustments required by all concerned were tremendous! Clearly, God's choice of me in that situation was not according to my experience or background but, in Paul's words, *"according to His own purpose and grace."*

Never limit God to what you believe you can do. Practically everyone in the Bible called by God for a special task felt incapable of fulfilling it. But God called them nonetheless. Whenever I meet a Christian who says, "God has called me to do this, and I know I can do it," I am almost positive God has not called that person to "do it." Our confidence in ourselves can be a disqualifier. Why? Because the Lord always requires us to operate not out of our strengths and abilities but out of His grace.

When we operate by His grace, we fulfill His purpose that we have been talking about. We become His chosen generation, His royal priesthood, His holy nation, His special people—His masterpiece!

11

REIGNING WITH CHRIST

We have seen that when we enter into a knowledge of God, we receive a greater understanding of our purpose in Him. In God's calling for us as His special possession to be a royal priesthood or a kingdom of priests, there are two facets involved: (1) we must be kings, and (2) we must be priests. This calling reflects God's intention from the beginning to share with mankind His dominion over the earth. In Genesis 1:26, the initial purpose of man's creation is stated:

> *Then God said, "Let Us make man in Our image, according to Our likeness; let them* [the human race] *have dominion...over all the earth."*

Because of Adam's disobedience to God (see Genesis 3), he and his descendants forfeited their position of dominion. Instead of reigning in obedience as kings, they were subjugated as slaves to sin and to Satan. However, the dominion that was lost to the whole race through Adam is restored to the believer in Christ:

> *For if by one man's offense* [that is, the offense of Adam] *death reigned through the one, much more those who receive abundance of grace and of the gift of righteousness will reign in life through the One, Jesus Christ.* (Romans 5:17)

The consequences of Adam's disobedience and of Christ's obedience are already manifested in this present life. Spiritual death now reigns over unbelievers, yet believers now reign in life by Christ. Through our union with Jesus, we have already been raised up to share the throne with Him, and we are reigning there with Him now.

Thus, God's redeeming grace lifts man from his position of slavery and restores him to his position of dominion. In the Old Testament, this is demonstrated in the deliverance of the Israelites from slavery in Egypt. In the New Testament, it is seen in our deliverance from sin and Satan, and also as we play our part in the double ministry of Christ: As kings, we rule with Him. As priests, we share His ministry of prayer and intercession. As we will discuss in more depth later, it is through prayer and intercession that we administer the authority that is ours in the name of Jesus.

A KINGDOM OF PRIESTS

A priest's function may be expressed using either a noun or a verb, and, in each case, it is precise. The noun is *sacrifice*—and it describes the one work that belongs exclusively to a priest. In the Bible, only priests are permitted to offer sacrifices. A priest's function is also expressed by the verb *offer*. As priests, we are responsible to *offer* sacrifices.

It is also important for us to recognize that, in a kingdom of priests, the only people who qualify to be in this kingdom are priests. Let me illustrate this concept with two examples. If we were talking about a race of giants, a person would need to be a giant to be part of that race. Or, if we were considering a society of botanists, a person would need to be a botanist to be considered for membership in that society. So, since the topic of our study is a kingdom of priests, may we agree that one must be a priest to be included in that kingdom?

In addition, I would like to point out that a person in this kingdom cannot become a king until they have learned to be a priest. We must never seek to separate these two functions from one another. If we would rule as kings, we must serve as priests. The practice of our priestly ministry is the key to the exercise of our kingly authority. A lack of living in this reality is one of the major problems with God's people. All of us would like to be kings, but few of us have mastered the duties of a priest. It is critical, therefore, for us to look closely into the particular ministry of a priest—which we learn very distinctly from the ministry of Jesus.

JESUS AS APOSTLE AND HIGH PRIEST

Hebrews 3:1 gives two titles to Jesus Christ:

> *Therefore, holy brethren, partakers of the heavenly calling, consider the Apostle and High Priest of our confession, Christ Jesus.*

The ministry and titles of Jesus given here, "*the Apostle and High Priest of our confession* [or what we state we believe]," are unfamiliar to many Christians. Jesus had twelve disciples, later called apostles (ones who were "sent"). But how many of us realize that Jesus Himself was the Apostle sent by God to all humanity for three and a half years? Following that time of being an Apostle, Jesus has been our High Priest for two thousand years!

In the Old Testament, specific instructions for priests are found in the book of Leviticus. However, much about the ministry and function of a new covenant priest is found in the epistle to the Hebrews. The revelation of the high priesthood of Jesus in Hebrews is unique in the New Testament and is of tremendous importance.

Few of us understand that, without a priest, we have no possibility of approaching almighty God. We cannot offer God a gift or bring God a sacrifice unless there is a priest to present it to Him. We tend to approach God with this attitude: "Here I am, God. Here's my offering. I hope You're glad to get it." That is not the way it is. The truth of the matter is, it is our profound privilege to be able to offer anything to God; and, again, we can't do so without a priest. In this regard, let's consider Hebrews 5:1:

> *For every high priest taken from among men is appointed for men in things pertaining to God, that he may offer both gifts and sacrifices for sins.*

Please notice once more that it is the duty of a priest to *offer*. Without a priest, we cannot offer a gift or sacrifice to God. We are totally dependent on our High Priest, Jesus, for this. Without Him, we would have no relationship, no communion, and no communication with God.

A CHOSEN PRIEST

In Hebrews 5:4, speaking about Christ in His earthly life, the author of Hebrews says this concerning the honor of being called High Priest:

> *No man takes this honor to himself, but he who is called by God, just as Aaron was.*

Aaron did not choose himself to be high priest; God chose Aaron for this position. When that choice was contested by some of the Israelite leaders, God said, in effect, "I'll settle the question once and for all." The Lord confirmed His choice of Aaron by causing Aaron's rod to bud, blossom, and bring forth almonds in twenty-four hours. (See Numbers 16–17.)

Even Jesus did not choose Himself to be High Priest, as we read in Hebrews 5:5:

> *So also Christ did not glorify Himself to become High Priest, but it was He* [God] *who said to Him: "You are My Son, today I have begotten You."*

Here, the writer of Hebrews is quoting Psalm 2:7, where God the Father is speaking to God the Son.

A PRIEST FOREVER

The writer continues with the same theme in Hebrews 5:6:

> *As He* [God] *also says in another place: "You are a priest forever according to the order of Melchizedek."*

According to Hebrews 5:5–6, God the Father not only declared Jesus to be His Son, but He also ordained Him as *"a priest forever according to the order of Melchizedek."* (We will talk about Melchizedek and his significance in the next chapter.)

Please note that because Jesus was a priest, He had to offer sacrifices; otherwise, He would not have been a priest. But because Jesus was not of the tribe of Levi, but rather of the tribe of Judah, He could not offer the animal sacrifices that were offered exclusively by the Levites. He was not, therefore, a Levitical priest. He had to offer another kind of sacrifice, which is described in Hebrews 5:7:

> *In the days of His flesh, when He had offered up prayers and supplications, with vehement cries and tears to Him who was able to save Him from death, and was heard because of His godly fear.*

In previous chapters, we discussed the fear of the Lord. Why was Jesus heard by His Father? Because He prayed out of "*His godly fear.*" In the days of His earthly ministry, Jesus offered up the sacrifice of prayers and supplications. These were not His final offering, as we will see in the next chapter. But the key phrase here is "*offered up.*" Jesus "*offered up prayers and supplications...to Him who was able to save Him from death.*" The Greek reads "out of death." We know that God did not keep Jesus from dying. However, He resurrected Him *out of* the dead.

This marks an important truth for our lives. There are times when we pray that the Lord will keep us safe from trouble. Even though God hears our prayers, He sometimes still permits us to go into a difficult situation. Then, later, He delivers us out of that situation. Why does He work in this way? Because He has something greater in mind for us—something that could not have been accomplished had we not gone through that situation.

In chapter 12, we will continue to explore aspects of the priesthood of Jesus so we may more fully understand our purpose in Christ as it relates to knowing God better.

12

OUR FORERUNNER

In an earlier chapter, we discussed the Holy of Holies, which lies beyond the second veil in the tabernacle. By virtue of His holiness and sacrifice on the cross, Jesus, our Forerunner, went behind the second veil into the immediate presence of God. The writer of Hebrews tells us that the hope generated by the work of Jesus is the anchor of our souls:

> *This hope* [which is *"set before us"* (verse 18)] *we have as an anchor of the soul, both sure and steadfast, and which enters the Presence behind the veil, where the forerunner has entered for us, even Jesus, having become High Priest forever according to the order of Melchizedek.*
>
> (Hebrews 6:19–20)

ANCHORED SECURELY

"This hope we have as an anchor of the soul" (Hebrews 6:19). Why does our soul need an anchor? Because the soul is like

a ship on the water. There is nothing in the water itself that will secure that ship. In order to secure itself, a ship must pass its anchor from the ship through the water, and then fasten it onto some immovable element, such as rock. You and I need an anchor for our souls. We are like ships in the water, with nothing stable in this temporal world on which to secure ourselves. If we want stability, we must pass our anchor of hope through our temporal world and into eternity. There, we anchor our hope within the second veil, where Jesus entered into the immediate presence of God. He is the Rock to which we are anchored. What a blessed thought!

Later portions of the book of Hebrews speak of faith and hope: *"Faith is the substance of things hoped for"* (Hebrews 11:1). Faith is in the present; hope is in the future. If you have faith, it is the basis for your hope. Our anchor, however, is not faith in the now. Our anchor is hope, which is in the future.

Some people live according to the materialistic claim that everything of value is in the here and now. That is an error! No matter how good we have it now, there is something better to come. If we become taken up with merely temporal concerns, we become like a ship without an anchor. Sooner or later, a storm will arise in our lives. When it does, we will discover that the only suitable anchor to hold us will be our connection with the stability of eternity.

This is a critical issue. We must not become solely preoccupied with day-to-day concerns, because our hope is in eternity. It is in eternity that we must have our strongest anchor. Why? Because this world is temporary and impermanent. As the writer of Hebrews declares, *"Here we have no continuing city, but we seek the one to come"* (Hebrews 13:14). Our hope lies in the future.

THE MYSTERY OF MELCHIZEDEK

Let us return to Hebrews 6:19–20 concerning the anchor of our soul and Jesus our Forerunner. It will serve as a helpful lead-in to our next topic as we continue to learn more about the significance of Jesus being our High Priest through whom we may enter God's presence.

> *This hope we have as an anchor of the soul, both sure and steadfast, and which enters the Presence behind the veil, where the forerunner has entered for us, even Jesus, having become High Priest forever according to the order of Melchizedek.*

When the writer refers to Jesus as the "*forerunner*" entering "*behind the veil,*" he means Jesus has gone there to prepare the way for us to be with Him. He has become "*High Priest forever according to the order of Melchizedek*" within the second veil, representing us before God and leading the way for us to follow Him there. Since we are to be a kingdom of priests, or kings and priests, we must understand the nature of "*the order of Melchizedek.*"

THE ORDER OF MELCHIZEDEK

The identity of Melchizedek remains a matter of discussion among Bible commentators—whether he was simply a preincarnate revelation of Jesus or whether he was an actual, real person named Melchizedek. (Personally, I don't know, and I am quite content to find out when I get to eternity!) We may never understand Melchizedek fully. Regardless, the Bible does reveal some interesting information about him. Hebrews 7:1–3 makes the following statements:

> *For this Melchizedek, king of Salem, priest of the Most High God, who met Abraham returning from the slaughter of the kings and blessed him, to whom also Abraham gave a tenth part of all, first being translated "king of righteousness," and then also king of Salem, meaning "king of peace," without father, without mother, without genealogy, having neither beginning of days nor end of life, but made like the Son of God, remains a priest continually.*

First, Melchizedek's very name means "*king of righteousness.*" In Hebrew, *melchi* means "king," and *zedek* means "righteousness." Second, Melchizedek was, by geographical location, the king of Salem (or Jerusalem), a place-name whose meaning corresponds to the modern Hebrew word *shalom,* which signifies "peace." Thus, he was both a king of righteousness and a king of peace. Finally, he was "*priest of the Most High God.*" Therefore, the two offices of king and priest were fulfilled by one person.

Melchizedek is first mentioned in Genesis 14:18, where we also see the first appearance of the word *priest* in the Scriptures:

> *Then Melchizedek king of Salem brought out bread and wine; he was the priest of God Most High.*

Usually, when an important concept is introduced in Scripture, the seed of truths that will be unfolded later is found in the first reference. So it is very important to see that Melchizedek was both a priest and a king, which was God's original intention for humanity. Later, under the law of Moses—an inferior arrangement suited to the people's weakness—the two functions of king and priest were separated. Priesthood went to the tribe of Levi, kingship to the tribe of Judah—and they were not allowed to be interchanged.

Two kings, Saul and Uzziah, did offer sacrifice, but God judged both of them for transgressing the law by exercising the function of a priest. Because of his transgression, Saul eventually lost his kingdom and his life. (See, for example, 1 Samuel 13:7–14.) Uzziah was struck with leprosy when he entered the temple to burn incense. (See 2 Chronicles 26:16–20.) These incidents highlight an important principle. We must never abrogate our God-ordained function, whatever it may be.

The priesthood of Melchizedek reappeared on the stage of human history at the coming of Jesus Christ —but with a difference. Previously, the Levitical priests had nothing to offer the people until the people first offered something to them. In other words, only when a person brought an offering for sacrifice could the priest give back part of it to the person who brought it. Let's remember, however, that Melchizedek offered Abraham bread and wine that Abraham had not first offered to him. As we recall regarding the Last Supper, when the meal was concluded, Jesus took the bread and the wine and gave them to His disciples. It was if He were saying, "Here is the priesthood of Melchizedek restored in Me."

Thus, when we are born again into the kingdom of God through faith in Jesus Christ, we do not come into the Levitical priesthood but into the priesthood of Melchizedek.

JESUS'S FINAL OFFERING

I realize that we are coming to some rather deep truths here. Let us trust that as we allow them to soak in, the Holy Spirit will help us to understand and utilize them in our lives. This applies to the principle we cover in this section. We will start with our earlier reminder that neither gifts nor sacrifices can be offered to God except through a priest. This brings us to Hebrews 8:3–4:

> *For every high priest is appointed to offer both gifts and sacrifices. Therefore it is necessary that this One* [Jesus] *also have something to offer. For if He were on earth, He would not be a priest, since there are priests who offer the gifts according to the law.*

As we observed earlier, Jesus did not offer animal sacrifices, nor did He need to, because priests from the tribe of Levi were already offering those. And as Hebrews 7:14 points out, Jesus came not from the tribe of Levi but from the tribe of Judah, which was the kingly tribe. But because He was a priest as well as a king, He had to present offerings, like every priest.

What did Jesus offer? We saw in Hebrews 5:7 that He offered prayers and supplications. But these were not His final offering. In Hebrews 9:13–14, we read what His final offering was:

> *For if the blood of bulls and goats and the ashes of a heifer, sprinkling the unclean, sanctifies for the purifying of the flesh, how much more shall the blood of Christ, who through the eternal Spirit offered Himself without spot to God, cleanse your conscience from dead works to serve the living God?*

What did Jesus offer? *Himself.* He was both priest *and* sacrifice. No other priest was qualified to fulfill both parts, and no other sacrifice would have been sufficient. On the cross, Jesus combined in Himself the roles of priest and sacrifice, which He did "*through the eternal Spirit.*"

A HELPFUL INSIGHT

Please allow me to explain why it is so important to me that the writer refers to *"the eternal Spirit"* (Hebrews 9:14). I have related this story in some of my other books, and it is particularly relevant to our topic here.

I vividly remember being confronted with the gospel, for the second time, when I was a corporal in the British Army in 1941. It was in a Pentecostal church in Scarborough, England. The first time had been the previous Sunday morning when I visited a church where the preacher asked people to raise their hands to accept the sacrifice of Jesus Christ on their behalf. I was indignant to be asked to do something so unbecoming and embarrassing as raising my hand in public. But as I sat there brooding over this insult, the Holy Spirit, to my intense shock, raised my hand for me. I was not only embarrassed about this situation but also somewhat scared.

Nothing much more developed in that service, but the preacher announced that the following Tuesday night, there was to be a revival at the Assemblies of God church. I had no idea what a "revival" was. But I thought, "Whatever this thing is that got started, I'll see it through." So, Tuesday night found me in the Assemblies of God church.

It was much the same kind of congregation as the Sunday before. Since it was wartime, it was mostly old ladies, and not many of them. But there I was, a soldier in uniform, sitting among them.

The speaker preached about Enoch: *"He was not; for God took him"* (Genesis 5:24 KJV). When he came to the end of his message, I knew what was going to happen, and I was on my guard. "Every head bowed, every eye closed," he said. I thought to myself, "The last time, Somebody else raised my arm for me." Since I could not expect that to happen twice, I put my arm up myself.

Once I put my arm up, the whole congregation seemed to breathe a sigh of relief. I must have been the only sinner in the place, and they had probably been waiting for me to respond. This time, the preacher came to speak with me. We looked one another up and down, and I think he knew I was going to be a problem.

He asked me two questions. The first one was, "Do you believe you're a sinner?" In my mind, I quickly went over every reasonable definition of *sinner*. Every one of them fit me exactly, so I said, "Yes, I believe I'm a sinner."

Then he asked, "Do you believe Jesus Christ died for your sins?"

"To tell you the truth," I replied, "I can't see what the death of Jesus Christ so many centuries ago could possibly have to do with the sins that I've committed in my lifetime." I could see no logical connection, no possible way that would make sense. Wisely, the preacher left me to God.

Thankfully, God dealt with me. About two days later, as I was reading my Bible, I discovered Hebrews 9:14, which answered my problem. It informed me that Christ *"through the eternal Spirit offered Himself without spot to God."* I knew that *eternal* meant "not within the limits and framework of time." Eternity was something outside of time, and Jesus had offered Himself *"through the eternal Spirit."* That day, the second question was settled for me, and I met the Lord.

In His death on the cross through the eternal Holy Spirit, Jesus encompassed the sins of all humanity—past, present, and future—in one single sacrifice of Himself. It was His final offering.

13

OUR PATTERN

If we are to be priests after the order of Melchizedek, in which Jesus is the great High Priest, then our priestly ministry must be patterned after Jesus's. From our earlier studies, we may recall the description of Jesus's priestly ministry—that He *"offered up prayers and supplications"* (Hebrews 5:7) and that He *"offered Himself without spot to God"* (Hebrews 9:14). In addition, Jesus, as well as the apostles, modeled and encouraged generous giving (see, for example, Luke 6:30; Galatians 2:10), which is described as a sacrifice in the book of Hebrews.

As priests of the New Testament, our ministry is *"to offer up spiritual sacrifices acceptable to God through Jesus Christ"* (1 Peter 2:5). Thus, in the same three distinct ways in which Jesus offered sacrifice, we must offer sacrifice. The first kind of sacrifice is *the offering of prayers,* which include praise, thanksgiving, supplication, intercession, petition, and everything else under the general activity of prayer. Many of the *"spiritual sacrifices"* offered up by Christians are the various forms of prayer. The second sacrifice is *the giving of our resources,* and the third is *the giving of ourselves.*

THREE KINDS OF SACRIFICE

In this section, we will cover in more detail the three areas of sacrifice we make in emulating Jesus, our Pattern.

1. THE OFFERING OF PRAYERS

The first sacrifice is titled "The Offering of Prayers," but, more accurately, it could be called "The Sacrifice of Praise." As we explore this sacrifice, let's begin with Hebrews 13:15:

> *Therefore by* [Jesus] *let us continually offer the sacrifice of praise to God, that is, the fruit of our lips, giving thanks to His name.*

Part of the all-inclusive word *prayers* is the sacrifice of praise. The above verse specifies both praise and giving thanks, which we are to offer continually. The life of the Christian should be a life of continuing praise and thanksgiving. These activities are not something we do merely when we come together in a church service; they should be the continual outflow of the divine life within us.

I have learned that if we want to keep the devil away, the best thing we can do is to praise God continually. The devil hates and fears praise as much as anything else you and I can do. So, when difficulties come, we should never clam up or shut ourselves in. We must not focus on ourselves and our problems because the more we focus on our difficulties, the worse they get. Rather, we turn our faces outward and lift every matter up to God. We begin to praise Him.

Let's remember, praise is a sacrifice. A sacrifice costs us something, or else it would not be a sacrifice. King David said, *"I will not offer burnt offerings to the Lord my God that cost me nothing"* (2 Samuel 24:24 NASB). Therefore, it is vital for you and me to praise God when we least feel like it. Those who praise God only on the basis of good feelings have not learned the priestly ministry. If we praise God only on that basis, then, when we are down, we will go further down. Praise must never depend upon our circumstances. We praise God because He is always worthy of praise. There is never a time when He is not worthy of praise. *"Great is the Lord, and greatly to be praised"* (Psalm 96:4 NASB).

Praise is the acknowledgment of God's *greatness.*

Worship is the acknowledgment of God's *holiness.*

Thanksgiving is the acknowledgment of God's *goodness.*

We are required to offer all these sacrifices. They are not optional; they are an integral part of the ministry of being a priest. All those who continue in praise, worship, and thanksgiving will live a life of victory!

2. THE GIVING OF OUR RESOURCES

The next sacrifice we offer as priests is to share generously with other people what God has given us to share. As I mentioned above, in the book of Hebrews, we see that this activity is clearly called a sacrifice:

> *But do not forget to do good and to share, for with such sacrifices God is well pleased.* (Hebrews 13:16)

If you and I want to please God and be priests in the order of Melchizedek, we must follow the pattern of our Lord Jesus in sacrificial giving to others. That giving may be in the form of our time, our gifts, our strength, or our finances. Remember, "*it is more blessed to give than to receive*" (Acts 20:35). If we are only receiving, then we are living on a lower level of blessing.

If you will allow me, I want to personalize the words of 2 Corinthians 9:8 so that we can repeat them as a confession:

> *God is able to make all grace abound toward* [me], *that* [I], *always having all sufficiency in all things, may have an abundance for every good work.*

Why does God make all grace abound toward us? Because it is more blessed to give than to receive. God wants every one of His children to live on the higher level of blessing. He doesn't wish us simply to be a sponge, absorbing everything we can get, and then having to be squeezed to give anything out. We shouldn't be like the Dead Sea, which only receives the water coming in but gives forth nothing, and therefore has no life in it. Rather, we should be like the Sea of Galilee, which both receives and gives, and therefore abounds with life of every kind.

Do you understand, dear reader, that this is the way grace works? It is not something we have earned; it is absolutely unearned. Grace is given to us so that we "*may have an abundance for every good work.*" I can't emphasize this point enough: grace is given not for us to abound in our own carnal self-indulgence but for every good work.

Let's remember what Ephesians 2:10 says:

> *We are His workmanship, created in Christ Jesus for good works, which God prepared beforehand that we should walk in them.*

3. THE GIVING OF OURSELVES

The ultimate sacrifice of giving, patterned on the sacrifice of Jesus, is the giving of *ourselves*. This obligation is presented clearly in Romans 12:1:

> *I beseech you therefore, brethren, by the mercies of God, that you present your bodies a living sacrifice, holy, acceptable to God, which is your reasonable service.*

The word *"service"* turns our minds immediately toward the priesthood and our own priestly service. Paul says this service is *"reasonable"*—that is, we can do no less. What is the sacrifice? It is the sacrifice of our bodies—exactly like the sacrifice of Jesus. Jesus offered His body on the cross, and we, too, are asked to offer our bodies.

Paul is precise in his language, however, when He calls for *"a living sacrifice."* He states this first of all to contrast our sacrifice with the sacrifices of the old covenant, which were killed. Second, he calls it a living sacrifice to distinguish it from the sacrifice of Jesus, who actually did die on the cross.

Even so, we are to offer our bodies to God in a similar way. Just as the Levitical priest placed the animal sacrifice on the altar, and just as Jesus allowed His body to be placed on the cross, so we are to offer our bodies to God.

Paul's command includes the word *"therefore."* (I like to say, "Whenever you find a *therefore,* you need to find out what it's there for.") This *therefore,* near the beginning of Romans 12, is there because of the preceding eleven chapters of Romans, which unfold the whole theological basis of the gospel. Romans is the great theological presentation of the gospel, setting forth mankind's need and God's complete provision for that need through the sacrifice of Jesus on the cross on our behalf.

Romans also addresses the difficult issues of predestination and divine election, which are worked out in chapters 9–11 in the context of God's dealings with Israel. Please bear in mind that God's dealings with Israel are not some postscript or addendum in history. They are an essential part of the basic revelation of the doctrine of the gospel. We cannot understand the gospel fully until we understand God's relationship with Israel as presented in Romans.

It is then, immediately after chapter 11, that Paul says, "*I beseech you therefore,...that you present your bodies a living sacrifice.*" In other words, in light of all God has done for us, what is our reasonable response? Paul says there is only one reasonable response: *we offer God our bodies.* At the end of this tremendous unfolding of the mercy of God throughout the book of Romans, we ask this question: "God, what do You want from me?" God responds, "Don't be super-spiritual; just give Me your body." This is our priestly work: offering our bodies as living sacrifices.

It is only after we have obeyed in making that sacrifice that God says, "Now that you have offered yourself, I will tell you some of the benefits."

SACRIFICE BRINGS CHANGE

In Romans 12:2, Paul offers us the benefits of sacrifice:

> *Do not be conformed to this world, but be transformed by the renewing of your mind, that you may prove what is that good and acceptable and perfect will of God.*

We are not to be like the people of this unregenerate world. We are to be different—not *conformed* but *transformed*. This is a transformation that takes place within us. Again, religion tries to change people through some outside influence—rules, standards, or more information. Grace, on the other hand, changes people from within.

Many people are involved in legalistic churches where everything is measured by external rules, often unspoken, defining what you must do to be a "good" Christian. This is the human way of trying to change. Legalism, whether in Judaism, Islam, or Christianity, approaches mankind from without. But God says, "Let Me change you from within; that will take care of the way you live. If I change the way you think, you will no longer live as people who think like the world do." God transforms us by changing our minds—and when our minds are changed, our lifestyle is changed. God's approach is more logical and practical.

It is clear from what Paul declares that God will not renew our minds until we have given Him our bodies. If we want our minds changed, we put our bodies on the altar, and then God will renew our minds. With our minds renewed, we *"may prove"*—or find out in experience—*"what is that good and acceptable and perfect will of God."*

It is tremendously important for us to understand that unless our minds are renewed, we cannot discover the will of God. God does not reveal His will to the unrenewed mind. Romans 8:7 tells us that *"the carnal mind is enmity against God."* God does not reveal His plans to those at enmity with Him. We must change our way of thinking before we can apprehend God's plan for our lives and deepen our knowledge of Him. He has good works prepared for us to walk in, but we cannot discover them until we have placed our bodies on the altar and, as a result, experienced the renewal of our minds.

THREE STAGES OF GOD'S WILL

Only when we come into God's presence solely because of who He is—not for what He can do for us—and present ourselves to Him unreservedly can we truly know Him and discover His will in three successive phases: good, acceptable, and perfect.

God's will is good. God never plans anything bad for any of His children. He never did and He never will.

God's will is acceptable. Once you and I begin to appreciate how good God's will really is, we will accept and embrace it.

God's will is perfect. God's will includes every area of our lives, every need and every situation.

Nothing happens by accident in the life of a child of God who is surrendered to the purposes of God—because *"all things work together for good to those who love God..."* (Romans 8:28). And we must not stop there! Paul continues in the rest of the verse, *"...to those who are the called according to His purpose."* When we are walking in the purposes of God and in our callings in Him, then, according to the love of God, everything works together for good in our lives.

As you read this now, you are faced with a challenge: Will you place your body on the altar of God's service without reservation?

You may have heard this biblical teaching before but never acted on it. Maybe you have never totally surrendered your body to God. If you decide to do so, it means you make no further determinations about your body—not what it eats, what it wears, where it goes, or the job that it does. The Lord decides all these things for you. You may end up working in Christian ministry, in a trade, in a profession, or as a homemaker, perhaps doing what you never expected or even going somewhere you never imagined. But that will be God's decision.

I want to further challenge you with this question: Are you prepared to let God have that much authority in your life? If you are, you will find it is the best decision you ever make, and one of your greatest steps ever toward truly knowing God.

Now that you have been confronted with God's requirement to offer Him your body as a living sacrifice, if you want to offer it to Him now, then tell Him so simply and sincerely with the following words:

> God, here I am. I place my body on the altar of Your service without reservation. From now on, it belongs to You. I offer it to You in Jesus's name. Amen.

Personal surrender opens the way into kingship. Only when we offer all three kinds of sacrifice—the offering of prayers, the giving of our resources, and the giving of ourselves—will we discover our identity as citizens of the kingdom of priests and holy nation God is calling forth. That destiny—our greatest calling and blessing—is the subject of our final chapters in this book.

14

DESTINED TO BE KINGS

The identity of God's people as a kingdom is a continuing theme that runs throughout the whole revelation of Scripture. We have seen that the Jewish people, before their deliverance from Egypt, were slaves. After their redemption, it was God's purpose for them to become kings. The same pattern is true for God's people today.

We have only two options: *we can live like slaves* or *we can live like kings*. For those who have been redeemed through Jesus Christ, God's divine purpose for them is to live like kings. But although their destiny is to be kings, many children of God are still living like slaves. They have not been renewed in their minds, they have not apprehended God's will, and they have not made the commitment to personal surrender, which opens the way into kingship. Theologically, these children of God are kings; but, experientially, they are slaves. The deciding difference, as we noted from the book of Daniel, is that those who live as kings are "*the people who know their God* [who] *shall be strong, and carry out great exploits*" (Daniel 11:32).

HEADS OR TAILS?

As we reviewed earlier, in Deuteronomy 28, the first fourteen verses describe the blessings we receive for hearing God's voice and doing what He says. In that list of blessings, Moses makes two simple but profound statements: "*The* L*ORD* *will make you the head and not the tail; you shall be above only, and not be beneath*" (verse 13). I have often reflected on what this means in the practical terms of daily living. May I ask you this, dear reader: Where are you living in terms of your current situation? Are you the head or the tail? Are you above or beneath your circumstances?

An amusing story is told of two Christians who greet each other on the street. The first asks the second, "How are you doing?"

The second replies, "Well, under the circumstances, not bad."

To which the first answers, "What are you doing under the circumstances?"

We are not called to be living "under" the circumstances. We are called to live above, not beneath. Practically speaking, the head makes the decisions, while the tail just gets dragged along. Which way describes the way you are living? Are you the decision-making part? Or are you the part that gets dragged around by circumstances, pressures, and forces you cannot control?

There is no middle ground between living like kings and living like slaves. We have invented a great deal of comfortable middle ground in our thinking and in our church life that does not exist in the Bible. Jesus said, *"He who is not with Me is against Me, and he who does not gather with Me scatters abroad"* (Matthew 12:30). There is only one choice in this relationship. If you are not with Jesus, you are against Him. And there is only one choice in the activity described. You can either gather, bringing in that which is positive, or you can scatter, squandering your time, talents, energy, and all that God has given you in unproductive, worthless activity. Each of us is in just one category or the other.

It is important, then, that we come to grips with our calling as kings and priests. This is our destiny, and not only God but also the world is waiting to see God's people become the kingdom of priests He is calling us to be.

Do you think the world is disappointed in the church? Society recognizes somewhat how the church should be. In fact, they can often point out her failures and inconsistencies better than we ourselves can. But if people in the world see a church that is ultimately not doing what it should, is it any wonder they disregard it? In a sense, the world is saying to us, "Why don't you people become what God intended you to be? We don't want theory. We want something that works in daily living."

When we in the church begin to function as kings and priests—not just in theology but also in experience—I believe we will see the fulfillment of the prophetic promises for a multitude of people coming into the kingdom of God.

UNDERSTANDING WHO WE ARE

As we saw previously, the king rules and the priest offers sacrifice. In order to be kings, we must learn to be priests because the kingdom of God is a kingdom of priests. Thus, if you and I do not know how to function as priests, we will not have the privilege of ruling as kings. Once more, the great barrier to the manifestation of the kingdom of God is the fact that God's people have not learned to function as priests.

As we also noted, the New Testament speaks of three sacrifices that we, as priests, must offer. First, we are to offer prayer—the sacrifice of our lips, which is praise and thanksgiving. Second, we are to offer the sacrifice of our giving and generosity—doing good and sharing with others out of what we possess and through the gifts we have been given. Our third and most important sacrifice is the placing of our bodies on the altar of God's service.

Remember, when we operate effectively as priests, we qualify to rule as kings. Or, to express it more simply and bring it down to a basic activity, *God has destined us to rule by prayer.* When we pray, we can begin to rule. In the next section, we will examine the first of two pictures that will help us visualize who we are as kings and priests. We will look at the second picture in the next chapter.

THE ASSEMBLY IN HEAVEN

Hebrews 12:22–24 gives us this magnificent picture:

> *But you have come to Mount Zion and to the city of the living God, the heavenly Jerusalem, to an innumerable company of angels, to the general assembly and church of the firstborn who are registered in heaven, to God the Judge of all, to the spirits of just men made perfect, to Jesus the Mediator of the new covenant, and to the blood of sprinkling that speaks better things than that of Abel.*

When the writer says, *"You have come,"* he speaks in the present perfect tense. What does this mean for us? It signifies that our coming to the city of God is not something that is *going to* happen; as far as God is concerned, it is something that *has already happened*. The writer is describing our spiritual location. Physically, as you read this, you may be in your living room or bedroom; there, in the body, you are located at some particular geographic point. But, spiritually, you have come to Mount Zion.

In a similar fashion, Paul writes that God *"made us alive together with Christ...and raised us up together, and made us sit together in the heavenly places in Christ Jesus"* (Ephesians 2:5–6). Paul does not say, "He is *going to* enthrone us" but "He enthroned us." The principle is: when you and I are identified with Jesus in His death and burial through baptism, we have followed Him legally and spiritually in every successive stage. We are made alive, we are resurrected, and we are enthroned.

This is the same principle we saw in chapter 9 with the tabernacle, where our destination is behind the second veil in the very presence of God. In Ephesians, our destination is ascension—to be kings and priests enthroned in the presence of God in heaven. Whichever way we approach this mystery, we end up at the same destination. We are in the presence of God as priests.

THREE SIGNIFICANT GROUPS ON MOUNT ZION

In the scene on Mount Zion from Hebrews 12, nine different elements are portrayed. We will not consider all of them but simply look at the three groups of created beings.

1. ANGELS

The end of Hebrews 12:22 mentions *"an innumerable company of angels."* I like that word *"innumerable"* because it portrays something powerful.

Many years ago, my wife Ruth and I were in Belfast, Northern Ireland, for six days of prayer with intercessors from all around the world. On the sixth day, as I was talking to a small group of leaders who had sponsored our meetings, Ruth saw heaven opened up before her, revealing a company of angels. There was no way, she said, to estimate the number of angels. They were all passing overhead, going from north to south, for a period she estimated to be ten minutes or so. As Ruth expressed, the word *innumerable* was just about the only word to describe what she saw. More exciting still was that some of these angels took a short stopover in Belfast to visit our meeting!

In the *New King James Version,* the next phrase, found in verse 23, reads, *"To the general assembly and church of the firstborn."* But the *New International Version* takes the term *general assembly* and attaches it to the angels. I am inclined to think that is probably the better translation. Verse 22 in the NIV reads, *"Thousands upon thousands of angels in joyful assembly."* When we see angels in any setting, it is impressive. But think about angels in joyful assembly!

2. THE CHURCH OF THE FIRSTBORN

Along with the angels is the *"church of the firstborn who are registered in heaven"* (Hebrews 12:23). This is the second group of created beings, the ones who are born again through faith in Jesus Christ.

3. SAINTS MADE PERFECT

Verse 23 of the same chapter in Hebrews mentions *"the spirits of just men made perfect."* These I understand to be the Old Testament saints who were not suddenly transferred from one kingdom to another by rebirth. These saints were *"made perfect"* by a lifetime walk of faith in God—and whose ultimate redemption comes through Christ, who died *"once for all"* (1 Peter 3:18 BSB). Some of the names of these saints are set forth in Hebrews chapter 11.

THE GREAT CELEBRATION

These, then, are the three companies of created beings in Mount Zion, the heavenly Jerusalem, in the very presence of God Himself. It is a glorious, majestic, powerful, and authoritative assembly. We could never count the millions and billions of beings in that assembly. This is the great celebration to which we *"have come,"* according to Hebrews 12:22—the celebration of all God's people destined to rule with Him.

Do we realize that, whenever we meet together with other believers in faith and in the name of Jesus, we are part of this assembly? Do we understand that, as God's people, we are part of this total assembly in Mount Zion? If we would realize and understand this, we would have a different attitude about assembling with our fellow believers. Most of the time, we merely say we are "going to church"—that is all it is. How much better to see ourselves taking our place in that glorious assembly in heaven!

15

PRIESTS AND RULERS LIKE JESUS

In our last chapter, we looked at the first of two pictures from Scripture that help us to visualize who we are as kings and priests. In this chapter, we will look at the second picture. This image comes from Psalm 110, one of the key passages about the high priesthood of Jesus in the order of Melchizedek. It is quoted more times in the New Testament than any other Old Testament passage, and it is one that Jesus actually applies to Himself.

ALREADY SEATED

In the first verse of Psalm 110, God the Father speaks to the Messiah, Jesus Christ the Son:

> *The* Lord *said to my Lord, "Sit at My right hand, till I make Your enemies Your footstool."*

"Sit at My right hand." We know that this is where Jesus is now—seated at God's right hand. The Scriptures place great emphasis on the fact that He is already seated. The writer of Hebrews contrasts Jesus with the Levitical priests, who remained standing, *"offering repeatedly the same sacrifices, which can never take away sins"* (Hebrews 10:11). The priests never sat down. Why did they stand? Because their job was never complete! In contrast, verse 12 goes on to say of Jesus:

> *But this Man, after He had offered one sacrifice for sins forever, sat down at the right hand of God.*

Why did Jesus sit down? Because He was never going to offer another sacrifice. His job was complete! Again, there is tremendous significance in the fact that Jesus is seated, and that He is seated on a throne—because He is a king as well as a priest.

The second verse of Psalm 110 is also key:

> *The* Lord *shall send the rod of Your strength out of Zion.*
> *Rule in the midst of Your enemies!*

These first two verses of Psalm 110, as I interpret them, involve all three persons of the Godhead. God the Father says to Jesus the Son, *"Sit at My right hand, till I make Your enemies Your footstool."* Then God the Holy Spirit sends the rod of Christ *"out of Zion"* to enable Him to rule in the midst of His enemies. That was accomplished—and Jesus is seated on the throne right now, ruling in the midst of His enemies. Jesus is never going to abdicate. His enemies have not yet all been made His footstool: they are still active, hateful, and vociferous. The earth is full of them, and they are increasing in number, activity, and malice. But Jesus is sitting on His throne and has chosen to rule by the rod of His authority, sent out of Zion by the Holy Spirit, enabling Him to rule in the midst of His enemies.

In fact, Jesus is actually ruling out of His people, that great assembly we talked about in the previous chapter. We, as the church—those who are born again through faith in Jesus Christ—are part of that assembly, along with the saints made perfect by their lifetime walk of faith. Angels—as the third company of created beings ruling in the earth today on behalf of Christ over His enemies—also have a part to play.

Various passages of Scripture confirm the tremendous task of believers to co-rule with Jesus, sharing the throne with Him. Romans 5:17, for example, says that *"those who receive abundance of grace and of the gift of righteousness will reign in life through the One, Jesus Christ."* This reigning does not only take place in heaven after we die. It also takes place right here in this present life. We are to reign on earth with Christ and share His authority—a truth we will see more clearly as this chapter unfolds.

It is our responsibility to bring Christ's enemies into subjection to the will of God so that God's plan for the nations may be worked out on earth. Jesus Christ is not going to do it in person; He has sat down in heaven. God the Father says, "I'm taking over now, and I will establish Your authority in the earth through My assembled people." Thus, by the power and direction of the Holy Spirit, the authority of Jesus Christ over the nations is going forth from God's people.

THE ROD OF STRENGTH

Next, let us explore what Psalm 110:2 means when it says that *"the LORD shall send the rod of Your strength out of Zion."*

A rod is the emblem of a ruler's authority and is often mentioned in the Old Testament. When the Israelites were enslaved in Egypt, God called Moses to go back to that land, where he had been raised, as His messenger to Pharaoh. But Moses replied, "I can't do it. Suppose Pharaoh says, 'Who sent you?' I have nothing to show him."

The Lord asked, "What do you have in your hand?"

"It's just my shepherd's rod. That's all."

"Moses, you don't realize what you have in your hand. Throw it down on the ground and see what happens."

So, Moses threw his rod down on the ground, and it became a snake. Moses ran from the very object he had just been holding in his hand. To him, it had only been a shepherd's staff. He did not realize its potential.

Then the Lord said to him, "Now pick up the snake by the tail."

Anyone who knows anything about snakes knows you never pick up a snake by the tail! You pick it up right behind the head so it cannot bite you. No doubt, Moses reached out his hand rather gingerly and grabbed hold of the snake by the tail, and it became a rod again. (See Exodus 4:1–5.)

In essence, the Lord was saying to Moses, "That's all you need—your shepherd's rod in your hand. Go back to Pharaoh and do what I tell you, and you will have all the authority you need to redeem My people out of Egypt."

At this point, according to Exodus, the staff in Moses's hand became the rod of God. So, Moses went back to the Egyptian court with his brother, Aaron, and told Pharaoh, "The Lord told me that you are to let His people go."

Pharaoh said, "Who is the Lord? I will not let Israel go." Instead of agreeing, he redoubled the Israelites' slave labor. (See Exodus 5:1–20.)

The next time Moses and Aaron approached Pharaoh with the same demand, he responded differently. In a vivid and interesting scene, recounted in Exodus 7:1–12, Pharaoh essentially replied in this way: "What evidence do you have?"

At God's direction, Aaron, who had been appointed by God as Moses's prophet, threw down his rod, and it became a snake.

You would think this would have convinced Pharaoh. It did not.

Pharaoh responded, "I'll call some of my magicians." Then he said to them, "This is what Moses and Aaron did. What can you fellows do?"

It is amazing, but they did the same. They threw down their rods, and the rods became snakes.

The devil has supernatural powers—we must be under no delusion about that. But there was a difference: Aaron's snake ate up the magicians' snakes.

Let's just picture this aftermath, imagining the scene: when everyone walked away from that encounter, the magicians had no staffs, while the staff of God's servants was stouter and stronger than before! It should be that way every time we confront the devil. He walks away with nothing, while we are stronger for the encounter!

THE EXERCISE OF AUTHORITY

Even that result did not satisfy hard-hearted Pharaoh. The next morning, when Aaron stretched out his rod over the waters of Egypt, turning them to blood, Pharaoh said to his magicians, "What about you?"

They said, "We can do the same." And they did. They turned the water into blood. So Pharaoh remained unmoved.

A week later, when Pharaoh continued his refusal to let God's people go, Moses said, "I will bring the frogs out." Moses had Aaron stretch out his staff, and frogs came out of the waters of Egypt.

Once more, Pharaoh said to his magicians, "What about you fellows?" They said, "We can do the same thing." And they did.

Next, God told Moses, and then Moses told Aaron, to strike the dust of Egypt and turn it into lice. Pharaoh turned to the magicians and said, "What about you?" Again, they tried to duplicate this miracle; but, this time, they couldn't. They told Pharaoh, "'*This is the finger of God.*' Now we know we're dealing with the real God." (See Exodus 7:13–8:19.)

As we keep track of what happened in the exodus, we remember that it was God who enabled Moses to take dominion over Egypt, over the gods of Egypt, and over Pharaoh. It was the exercise of the authority of that rod that opened the way for the redemption of God's people out of Egypt.

THE AUTHORITY WE CARRY

By putting Christ's rod into our hands, God has authorized us to deal with the world around us. He has commissioned us to take dominion over this world, over its gods, and over its governments. Ours is not an authority to do arbitrarily whatever we feel disposed to do. Instead, we are given the authority to see the purposes of God for His people brought to fulfillment.

If Moses had not learned to use the rod of God, Israel would never have gotten out of Egypt. Similarly, until the church learns to use the authority committed to her through Jesus Christ, the purposes of God for the church will never come to fulfillment. It is the rod, the emblem of God's authority, that makes the difference.

Later on in Israel's journey from Egypt to the promised land, some of the Israelite leaders challenged the leadership of Moses and Aaron (see Numbers 16–17), an incident we looked at briefly in an earlier chapter. The Lord told Moses, "I'm going to settle this question once and for all. Tell the leader of every tribe to bring his staff and write his name on it. Then take all of the staffs, put them in the tabernacle in front of the Holy of Holies, and leave them there." Moses did exactly as he was told.

The next day, when Moses went to collect the rods, eleven of them were unchanged, but the twelfth staff had budded, blossomed, and brought forth almonds. The name on that rod was "Aaron." So God said, in effect, "Now we all know who the leader and high priest is."

The budding, blossoming, and fruit-bearing of the rod in twenty-four hours, which vindicated Aaron, is a type of resurrection. In the same way, by resurrecting Jesus, God vindicated Him as Messiah and Son of God. In the opening passage of his letter to the Romans, Paul speaks of this vindication:

> *...the gospel of God which He promised before through His prophets in the Holy Scriptures, concerning His Son Jesus Christ our Lord, who was born of the seed of David according to the flesh, and declared to be the Son of God with power according to the Spirit of holiness, by the resurrection from the dead.* (Romans 1:1–4)

"The Spirit of holiness" is a Hebrew expression for the Holy Spirit. What is the significance of the use of this term here? It is that Jesus did not raise Himself from the dead. The Holy Spirit, at the Father's direction, was the power that raised Him. That act declared Jesus to be the Son of God. It was the "budding" of the rod of Christ, which settled forever the issue of His eternal role as our High Priest.

OUR SUCCESSION

Revelation 1:5–6 shows us a beautiful picture of the succession in our priesthood, including an affirmation of the rulership of Jesus, whose authority we exercise on earth. The Holy Spirit refers to Jesus Christ as *"the faithful witness, the firstborn from the dead, and the ruler over the kings of the earth"* (verse 5). Please note the three successive phases. First, Jesus was *"the faithful witness."* He spoke the truth of God without compromise—without adding to it, without taking from it. Second, because Jesus was the faithful witness, God vindicated His witness by raising Him from the dead, making Him *"the firstborn from the dead."* Third, as the firstborn from the dead, Jesus is also *"the ruler over the kings of the earth."* Let's take note of that order again: the faithful witness, the firstborn from the dead, then the ruler of the kings of the earth.

The passage continues, giving us the connection to our priesthood and rulership in the pattern of Jesus: *"To Him who loved us and washed us from our sins in His own blood, and has made us kings and priests to His God and Father"* (verses 5–6).

What is our destiny as people who know their God and are continuing to seek out His mysteries? It is to enter the same ministries of king and priest that came to Jesus when He was raised from the dead and exalted at God's right hand. The authority is in the name that is on His rod, just as it was with Aaron. When we, by the Holy Spirit, stretch out the rod with the name of Jesus on it, we are exercising His authority over the nations.

16

RULING WITH JESUS'S AUTHORITY

The principles we covered in the previous chapter are of profound importance to our destiny as kings and priests to our God. Let's continue our study of this vital subject by returning to Psalm 110 for another look at the first two verses:

> *The* Lord *said to my Lord, "Sit at My right hand, till I make Your enemies Your footstool." The* Lord *shall send the rod of your strength out of Zion.* (Psalm 110:1–2)

To summarize, at the Father's direction, the Holy Spirit will send the rod of Jesus's authority—which has His name on it—out of Zion, the assembly of God's people as they gather together in Him. By this authority, exercised by the church, Jesus Christ will rule in the midst of His enemies.

REPRESENTATIVES OF JESUS

I trust you are grasping this profound truth. Jesus is seated in heaven and has, for the time being, finished His task. Now it is up to us. It is we, as we increase in our knowledge of God and enter into our calling, who must exercise the authority that has been vested in Him.

At the end of Matthew 28, Jesus said, *"All authority has been given to Me in heaven and on earth"* (verse 18). That leaves out nothing and no one! Then He said, *"Go therefore..."* (verse 19). In other words, "On the basis of the authority that has been given to Me, you must go." We go as His representatives, carrying and demonstrating His authority. The world will not know the authority that Jesus has until we go out and demonstrate it. He already has the authority, but its exercise and demonstration are our responsibility.

VOLUNTEERS FOR JESUS

Another principle emerges for us from verses 3 and 4 of Psalm 110:

> *Your* [God's] *people shall be volunteers in the day of Your power; in the beauties of holiness, from the womb of the morning, You have the dew of Your youth. The* L*ORD* *has sworn and will not relent* [or repent], *"You are a priest forever according to the order of Melchizedek."*

Everything predicted in these verses is tied to the fact that Jesus is the High Priest and King in the order of Melchizedek. The Hebrew word translated as *"power"* here is the modern Hebrew word for "army." It is the same word used in the phrase "the Lord of Hosts." God is *the Lord of Armies*.

The first part of verse 3 can be translated more literally, "Your people shall be freewill offerings in the day of Your army." There will be a day when God assembles His troops (the Lord's army) for the final conflict. God's people at that time will be set apart by one fact: they will be freewill offerings. This is the same truth we saw in Romans 12:1: *"Present your bodies a living sacrifice."* God is not after our time, our talents, or our money. What He wants is *you and me*. When He has *us*, He has our time, our talents, and our money. We must never offer Him anything else until we have first offered Him ourselves.

In Psalm 110:3, David also writes, *"In the beauties of holiness, from the womb of the morning, You have the dew of Your youth."* In the margin of the *New International Version*, a correct alternate translation for the last part of this verse reads, "Your young men will come to you like dew."

Let's think deeply upon the pictures presented here. First, *"the beauties of holiness,"* which I believe must be restored to the church. Contrary to what many people believe, holiness does not come from works. It comes by complete surrender, which is the ultimate sacrifice we are to offer as priests.

When David refers to *"the womb of the morning,"* the *womb* speaks of birth, and the *morning* speaks of the dark night that precedes it. We have the picture, therefore, of a period of darkness ending in a birth that brings forth a new day. In this new day, God the Father says to the Messiah, Jesus Christ the Son, "Your young men will come to You like dew."

One major emphasis of the Holy Spirit today is the calling of young people to be freewill offerings in the army of the Lord. The Lord is assembling His army to storm the stronghold of Satan and proclaim the gospel of the kingdom to every nation on earth. This beautiful psalm is a prophetic picture of God's intention.

INTERCESSORS FOR JESUS

There are two main elements in Psalm 110:2–3: the army that goes forth and the assembly that stretches out the rod of authority over the nations. This rod, I believe, is primarily the ministry of intercession. In this passage, we have a beautifully balanced picture of the two great thrusts of God's people taking the kingdom to the nations. First are the intercessors extending the rod of God, the one with Jesus's name on it, and bringing the nations into subjection to the purposes of God. Second, there are the young men and women who are freewill offerings to take the gospel of the kingdom everywhere God sends them.

I was deeply involved with the Jesus People movement in the 1960s in the United States. As always with such movements, there were some missteps among those who participated in it, but it was nonetheless a sovereign act of God. I got to know certain of the young people in this movement, some of whom are now grown-up and have become close friends and associates. In the early days, these dear young people would do anything and go anywhere. If they were in a Southern state and felt God wanted them in Alaska, they did not wait for money or transportation; they just set out for Alaska! That is the kind of attitude God is looking for in the day of His power.

In stark contrast to this kind of willingness, I see two main problems with most of the church today: self-centeredness and materialism. These attitudes have the potential to completely hinder the outworking of God's purposes. The Lord is looking for "freewill offerings," released from both self-centeredness and materialism. Potentially, the church already has the resources to finish the job of taking the kingdom to the nations. It is not resources we need. It is the willingness among us to go in obedience and release those resources wherever and however God directs.

PREPARING THE WAY

The last three verses of Psalm 110 speak about God's personal intervention at the close of this age. In my understanding, it is not the church that will establish the fullness of God's kingdom on earth. The church will *prepare the way* for the establishment of the kingdom of God on earth. Only Jesus can establish the kingdom. Some very good Bible teachers do not see it this way. But, in my view, there is an abundance of Scriptures that indicate it will take the Lord's intervention to finish the job.

In Psalm 110:5, we see again that Jesus has been seated at the Father's right hand:

> *The Lord is at Your right hand; He shall execute kings in the day of His wrath.*

The word translated "*execute*" here means "break in pieces." There is coming a day of God's wrath—let us have no misapprehension about that. God will judge the wicked—those people who will not submit to the righteous government of God, no matter how clearly it has been explained or demonstrated to them.

When I was a soldier in the British Army, I was traveling by train through the Sudan on a military assignment. As I was riding north from Khartoum, I came to a railway station at Atbara. The platform was alive with camels, donkeys, chickens, and other animals. There were young men and women, old men and women, boys, girls, and nursing infants. The platform was so crowded you could hardly separate one person from the next.

As I looked out, I said to myself casually, "I wonder what God thinks of all those people?" I received an immediate answer, as clear and as specific as I could ever hope for. Interestingly, I was not even asking for an answer! This was the response I sensed from the Lord: *Some weak, some foolish, some proud, some wicked, and some exceeding precious.*

I have never been able to improve on that classification. Some people never come into the kingdom because they are weak. Some never come because they are foolish. Some never come because they are proud. And some never come because they are just plain wicked. But, in the midst of it all, there are those who are "exceeding precious" who will come into the kingdom.

DIVINE INTERVENTION

It takes God to deal with the wicked—and, for my part, I am willing to let Him do it! If someone wants to be a hero and confront the Antichrist, he or she is welcome to it. But don't call me in. The Scriptures indicate that the Lord is going to lead His armies in battle from heaven in the final conflict; and, as I mentioned earlier, I believe it will take the Lord Himself to finish the matter.

I am looking for the Lord's return. I long for Him. I believe nothing but His return can solve the problems of humanity. Just to name one horrific dilemma, millions of people are dying every year of starvation, most of them children. But humanity, because of our confused and limited nature, lacks the capacity to solve these problems. Only one Person can solve them, and that is Jesus.

When He comes, He will take the five loaves and two fish and feed the starving multitudes. He will set up the kingdom of God, which will be ordered, righteous, and peaceful. In the meantime, you and I are the firstfruits of that kingdom, its demonstration on earth right now. Once more, our task is to prepare the way for the coming of the King, but we cannot substitute anything else for His coming.

We look again at Psalm 110:5:

> *The Lord is at Your right hand; He shall execute* [or break in pieces] *kings in the day of His wrath.*

I can only say, "Praise God!" Many of the "kings" of this world today need to be broken in pieces. The world has too many self-centered tyrants, warlords, and gangsters who are oppressing the poor, the innocent, and the defenseless. God may plan to save many of these tyrants. Who can say? But if they do not yield to the purposes of God, they will end up being broken in pieces.

The next section, verse 6, conveys the serious nature of God's intervention:

> *He shall judge among the nations, He shall fill the places with dead bodies, He shall execute the heads of many countries.*

This sounds to me like divine intervention on a major scale. But first we must do our job. Jesus said, "*This gospel of the kingdom will be preached in all the world as a witness to all the nations, and then the end will come*" (Matthew 24:14). This commission is as clear as anything the Lord ever said. The end cannot come until we have proclaimed the gospel of the kingdom to all nations. Until we do, we are delaying the return of Jesus Christ.

No brilliant program will ever be a substitute for Jesus's return. Rather, we must get moving and do the job we are supposed to be doing. The church is not called to be a super-government, nor are we a substitute for the fullness of the kingdom of God. Our job is to prepare the way of the Lord by demonstrating the kingdom in our relationships with God and with one another—in our holiness, in our authority, and in our love for one another and a lost world.

17

TEN FORCES OPPOSING GOD

It should be absolutely clear to us from what we covered in the previous chapter that we have a job to do—extending the rod of God's authority. I mentioned earlier that one major aspect of this job is our role as intercessors.

As a logical result of establishing a kingdom of priests, God wants to bring forth out of this generation an army of intercessors. If that does not happen, we will have missed a critical element in preparing for the coming of the kingdom.

I noted previously that Ruth and I attended an international conference of intercessors in Belfast, Northern Ireland. During this conference, we had reports from representatives of all areas of the earth except for South America. From their different backgrounds, all these representatives spoke about the main forces opposing God and His purposes in the earth.

After hearing these reports, I compiled a list of ten major evil forces at work almost universally throughout the world. I share them now because understanding these forces is relevant to our role of priestly intercession. These concerns are not necessarily listed in their order of importance, although I believe the first one is the root of all the other problems. It may surprise you.

1. A RESURGENCE OF THE OLD "GODS"

Remarkably, a resurgence of belief in the old "gods" is happening in many parts of the world. I read an article in a New Zealand airline magazine that spoke about an exhibition in New York introducing the Maori culture, which included much of their religion and beliefs. The reemergence of the Maori culture in New Zealand is one of the clearest examples of the resurgence of the "old gods" that ruled those islands. It is as if those "gods" are saying, "You haven't finished with us. You've driven us back, but you haven't cast us down. This is our land."

The same phenomenon is taking place, astonishingly, in the United States, Canada, Great Britain, Germany, and many other nations. In Scandinavia, it is the old Nordic gods that are reemerging. In Germany, it is the gods that are somehow associated with Richard Wagner's operas. In England, the resurgence of Druidry, or Druidism, is astounding. Having been born British and grown up there, I would not have believed that, in modern times, we would see Britishers actually practicing Druidry once again. These "gods"—evil supernatural forces and influences opposed to God—which Paul called *"principalities and powers"* (see, for example, Ephesians 3:10; Colossians 2:15), were driven back by the arrival of Christianity. But they have never been overthrown. As a result, they are now exploiting the rebelliousness of modern mankind to reassert their dominion.

In reality, when you go to the root of spiritual problems in most nations, a major factor is rebellion. It is interesting that, in every case, there is a link with ancient Babylon, *"the Mother of Harlots and of the Abominations of the Earth"* (Revelation 17:5).

2. APOSTASY AND DIVISION

I believe we are living in the time in history that Paul calls *"the falling away"* (2 Thessalonians 2:3) or *"the apostasy"* (verse 3 NASB). There have been wicked church leaders in every century, but only in the last one hundred years or so have recognized leaders of major denominations declared emphatically that they reject the basic truths of the Christian revelation: the virgin birth, the deity of Jesus, His substitutionary atonement, and His physical resurrection.

One Anglican priest, the Rev. David Jenkins, declared at one point that he did not believe any of those "theories"—and thereafter he was ordained the Anglican bishop of Durham by the Archbishop of Canterbury, who knew what the priest believed (or didn't believe). Mr. Jenkins had to declare on oath that he affirmed the Thirty-Nine Articles of Religion defining the biblical beliefs of the Church of England, although I doubt whether he believed many or most of them.

This is but a single graphic case in point. What has been happening in the church over the last century is without parallel in history. Ironically, the site of the origin of liberal theology is Germany, which gave birth to the Reformation five hundred years ago. But, in modern times, apostasy has spread from that nation like a cancer throughout the professing church all over the world.

Side-by-side with the issue of apostasy, the other problem in the church is division between true believers. Divisions and schisms were problems Paul confronted continually, and they are one of Satan's chief schemes to keep the church powerless and ineffective.

3. THE OVERTHROW OF LAW AND ORDER

The overthrow of law and order can be expressed in one word used by Jesus: *"lawlessness."* He said, *"Because lawlessness will abound, the love of many will grow cold"* (Matthew 24:12). Lawlessness is also expressed in two words that have come into wide usage in contemporary times, with all of our great scientific and social "progress": *terrorism* and *holocaust*. Another word, which was actually coined in the twentieth century, is *genocide*. This word did not exist in the English language until 1944. How much progress does that indicate?

When Satan wants to undermine authority, one of his tactics is to point out all the weaknesses and failings of authority. If that strategy doesn't work, the enemy pushes upon us the impression that if some other authority takes over, it will be better. However, in fact, it is often worse. This was the tactic behind the Russian Revolution in 1917 and the takeover of the German government by Hitler in the 1930s.

4. SELF-DESTRUCTION

Another feature of demonic activity in our day is self-destruction. This force makes some children bang their heads against walls, beat their own faces with their fists, cut into their flesh, or engage in other kinds of self-inflicted injury or self-mutilation. Incidents of the ultimate form of self-destruction—suicide—have skyrocketed among young people.

Demonic self-destruction is clear in many other examples. Especially during the time of World War II, it was very strong in Germany. Its citizens destroyed themselves following the spirit of Nazi racism and national pride. The same was true of the people of Japan. In modern times, we see this kind of self-destructive behavior in terrorists and proponents of radical Islam.

When a spirit of self-destruction grips individuals and nations, they will plunge themselves to destruction following some idea or vision, regardless of the consequences. This trait is evident as well in self-indulgent economic policies and the embracing of degenerate lifestyles.

5. PERMISSIVENESS, LICENTIOUSNESS, AND MATERIALISM

The dividing line between the world and the church today is hard to distinguish because the church has failed to maintain clear standards and has accepted what the world offers lying down. For example, pornography is a problem not only in the world but also in the church. It is readily available on the Internet. Additionally, American movies promote sexual promiscuity, perversion, vile language, and every kind of violence. Sadly, viewership of such content is not restricted to the world only; Christians are also watching it. Flagrant homosexuality and gender confusion are not only accepted as normal in secular society and in some sectors of the church, but they are also promoted, celebrated, and even taught in public schools to children of younger and younger ages.

Moreover, not only is divorce common in Western Europe and North America, but many people hardly take the trouble to get married anymore, living together without the benefit of covenant.

Materialism has become a religion in the West and in much of the rest of the world. People are no longer judged by their character but by their houses, their cars, their clothes, and their wealth.

6. AN UPSURGE IN THE OCCULT

Satanism, witchcraft, fortune-telling, Freemasonry, and other forms of dark spiritual activity are widely accepted in society today. Such practices are regarded as legitimate recreational or even spiritual pastimes, often advanced by television programs and popular movies. Many times, they are accepted even by Christians. Yet they are expressly forbidden by God in the Scriptures, and the warning about them is that involvement with such practices leads to physical and spiritual death.

7. ANTI-SEMITISM

Anti-Semitism is on the rise in our modern societies. Additionally, there is a powerful anti-Semitic element in the background of Christian theology and history. Whether we are aware of it or not, the church in Europe over the centuries has been the leader in anti-Semitism. Even the responsibility for the Holocaust lies at the door of the professing church in Europe. The growing incidence of anti-Semitism we see today is simply the culmination of what the church has sown for many centuries through the teachings of church leaders like Martin Luther and others.

The rising anti-Israel sentiment in the world and in the United Nations can only be described as supernatural. No matter what Israel does, she is condemned, while her enemies, even in the halls of academia, are generally allowed to do and say whatever they please.

8. SECULAR HUMANISM

The philosophy of secular humanism has been and continues to be rampant around the world. It is a "religion" that replaces God with no religion. In actual fact, it is just as much a religion as Christianity is. Basically, it makes humanity god, saying that "man is the measure of all things." Secular humanism declares that we do not need any form of deity to reach our full potential as human beings. By and large, secular humanism is the basis of the entire educational system of Western society today.

9. MARXISM

Marxism as a defined movement is not as strong now as it was when this list was first compiled. Even so, Marxist ideology, cloaked in the guise of social justice, is seeping into the thought processes and ideologies of many people, including in the universities. Its spiritual force thrives in the form of progressive socialism, which continues to enslave much of the West as one of the dominating forces of secular humanism, the previous issue on the list.

10. ISLAM

Islam is becoming a growing influence throughout the earth. Every culture in the world is, to one degree or another, threatened by it. Muslims are as committed as Christians are—if not more so—to reaching the uttermost parts of the earth with their religion.

At its root, Islam is radically anti-Semitic and anti-Christian, and it seeks to impose Sharia law (rulings based on Islamic scriptures) on the entire world. Most Christians believe the lie that Islam is a peaceful religion and do not realize that it identifies all non-Muslims as infidels and unbelievers worthy of death. I have lived among Muslims and learned to speak Arabic. From my knowledge of Islam and its fervor, I would say that there is no force in the world more cruel, more wicked, and more opposed to God and His people than Islam.

AN INCENTIVE TO INTERCEDE

I realize that this list of ten issues and problems facing us is rather daunting. It may even be discouraging. My hope, however, is that it is a helpful platform for our final chapter—and a positive incentive for us to step into our role as kings and priests.

18

CARRYING THE GOSPEL OF THE KINGDOM

We began this book with a reference to Daniel 11:32: "*The people who know their God shall be strong, and carry out great exploits.*" In the face of the challenging list in the previous chapter, it is self-evident that our quest to know God is not solely for the blessings it brings to us personally. Knowing God carries with it the commission to carry the gospel of His kingdom to all nations.

BATTLING FOR HEARTS AND MINDS

In the final analysis, the ten evil forces described in chapter 17 represent key strongholds Satan has constructed in people's minds. In a word, they are ideologies, which is another key word popularized in the twentieth century. *Ideology* refers to any set of beliefs or ideas. An ideology can be a stronghold of Satan built in the minds of men and women to prevent the gospel from taking effect. Every major dictatorship of the last century was built on an ideology. The aim: to captivate the minds of those who were ruled so no other source of information or direction could influence them.

Because these ten evil forces are significant strongholds, they are enemies that the church must combat through intercession and prayer. Only the body of Christ can cast down such strongholds and change the course of events. We alone possess the spiritual weapons that can actually break through the strongholds and expose the minds of men and women to the truth of the gospel. The gospel—and the gospel alone—has the power to pull people out of the captivity of Satan and into the freedom of the captivity of obedience to Jesus Christ.

This possibility and hope in our battle for the hearts and minds of men and women is best expressed by Paul in 2 Corinthians 10:3–5:

> *For though we walk in the flesh, we do not war according to the flesh. For the weapons of our warfare are not carnal but mighty in* [through] *God for pulling down strongholds, casting down arguments and every high thing that exalts itself against the knowledge of God, bringing every thought into captivity to the obedience of Christ.*

We are fighting a war against an unseen kingdom that seeks to dominate humanity with darkness and deception. The battlefield—as revealed in verse 5 just above—is the mind of humanity. The strongholds that reside there are raised up *"against the knowledge of God."*

Thus, we and all the church are engaged in a vast, intense conflict raging in the unseen world to capture the mind of the human race. Everything Satan does is an effort to keep all humanity—and, indeed, you and me—from coming into a personal, experiential knowledge of God. Satan knows that if he can keep men and women separated from the true knowledge of God, he has won an enormous victory.

INTERVENING IN THE UNSEEN REALM

Only when we grasp the truth that ultimate reality is unseen can we engage in effective intercession. This realization is clearly expressed by Paul in 2 Corinthians 4:17–18:

> *For our light affliction, which is but for a moment, is working for us a far more exceeding and eternal weight of glory, while we do not look at the things which are seen, but at the things which are unseen. For the things which are seen are temporary, but the things which are not seen are eternal.*

True reality, Paul is saying, is invisible and eternal. What most human beings consider "real"—the visible, material world—is only *temporarily* real. The invisible spiritual realm is the ultimate, permanent reality. The essence of intercession, then, is to intervene in the unseen world and contend with unseen spiritual realities.

Ephesians 6:12 says:

> *For we do not wrestle against flesh and blood, but against principalities, against powers, against the rulers of the darkness of this age, against spiritual hosts of wickedness in the heavenly places.*

Here is my own translation of this verse:

> Our wrestling match is not against persons with bodies, but against rulers with various areas and descending

> orders of authority, against world dominators of this present darkness, against spiritual forces of wickedness in the heavenlies.

Are you ready to answer the call to intercede as a king and a priest? Are you ready to do battle for people's hearts and minds?

OUR GREATEST CALLING

As I reminded us at the start of this chapter, we began this book with inspiring words from Daniel. Regarding the final great conflict of the age about which he prophesied, Daniel said, "*The people who know their God shall be strong, and carry out great exploits*" (Daniel 11:32).

Let us keep in mind that coming to know God is not just to make us feel good about ourselves; and accomplishing "*great exploits*" does not mean merely filling our lives with the blessings of God. Only when we know God personally can we become the special people He created us to be—a kingdom of priests and a holy nation. Only then can we fulfill these dual mandates of the church: intercession and evangelism.

In the words of Hosea 6:3 (NASB), then, "*let's press on to know the Lord.*" As we conclude this book, would you like to "volunteer freely" to do what Hosea is urging us to do? Would you pray with me now?

> Lord, my chief desire in life is to know You and to serve You. I offer myself now as a living sacrifice to You and Your purposes. By faith, I step into Your calling for me to be part of Your special people, Your kingdom of priests, Your holy nation.

I make myself available to You: use me and employ me in any area of service to You and Your kingdom, whether it be the sacrifice of prayer and praise or of giving or of simply laying down my life and my preferences to do Your will.

I am Yours, Lord—and, as a living sacrifice, I yield myself completely to You. In Jesus's name, amen.

ABOUT THE AUTHOR

Derek Prince (1915–2003) was born in India of British parents. He was educated as a scholar of Greek and Latin at Eton College and King's College, Cambridge, in England. Upon graduation, he held a fellowship (equivalent to a professorship) in Ancient and Modern Philosophy at King's College. Prince also studied Hebrew, Aramaic, and modern languages at Cambridge and the Hebrew University in Jerusalem. As a student, he was a philosopher and a self-proclaimed agnostic.

While serving in the Royal Army Medical Corps (RAMC) during World War II, Prince began to study the Bible as a philosophical work. Converted through a powerful encounter with Jesus Christ, he was baptized in the Holy Spirit a few days later. Out of this encounter, he formed two conclusions: first, that Jesus Christ is alive; second, that the Bible is a true, relevant, up-to-date book. These conclusions altered the whole course of his life, which he then devoted to studying and teaching the Bible as the Word of God.

Discharged from the army in Jerusalem in 1945, he married Lydia Christensen, founder of a children's home there. Upon their marriage, he immediately became father to Lydia's eight adopted daughters—six Jewish, one Palestinian Arab, and one English. Together, the family saw the rebirth of the state of Israel in 1948. In the late 1950s, they adopted another daughter while Prince was serving as principal of a teachers' training college in Kenya.

In 1963, the Princes immigrated to the United States and pastored a church in Seattle. In 1973, Prince became one of the founders of Intercessors for America. His book *Shaping History Through Prayer and Fasting* has awakened Christians around the world to their responsibility to pray for their governments. Many consider underground translations of the book as instrumental in the fall of communist regimes in the USSR, East Germany, and Czechoslovakia.

Lydia Prince died in 1975, and Prince married Ruth Baker (a single mother to three adopted children) in 1978. He met his second wife, like his first wife, while she was serving the Lord in Jerusalem. Ruth died in December 1998 in Jerusalem, where they had lived since 1981.

Until a few years before his own death in 2003 at the age of eighty-eight, Prince persisted in the ministry God had called him to as he traveled the world, imparting God's revealed truth, praying for the sick and afflicted, and sharing his prophetic insights into world events in the light of Scripture. Internationally recognized as a Bible scholar and spiritual patriarch, Derek Prince established a teaching ministry that spanned six continents and more than sixty years. He is the author of more than eighty books, six hundred audio teachings, and one hundred video teachings, many of which have been translated and published in more than one hundred languages. He pioneered teaching on such groundbreaking themes as generational curses, the biblical significance of Israel, and demonology.

Prince's radio program, which began in 1979, has been translated into more than a dozen languages and continues to touch lives. Derek Prince's main gift of explaining the Bible and its teachings in a clear and simple way has helped build a foundation of faith in millions of lives. His nondenominational, nonsectarian approach has made his teaching equally relevant and helpful to people from all racial and religious backgrounds, and his messages are estimated to have reached more than half the globe.

In 2002, he said, "It is my desire—and I believe the Lord's desire—that this ministry continue the work, which God began through me over sixty years ago, until Jesus returns."

Derek Prince Ministries continues to reach out to believers in over 140 countries with Derek's teaching, fulfilling the mandate to keep on "until Jesus returns." This is accomplished through the outreaches of more than forty-five Derek Prince offices around the world, including primary work in Australia, Canada, China, France, Germany, the Netherlands, New Zealand, Norway, Russia, South Africa, Switzerland, the United Kingdom, and the United States. For current information about these and other worldwide locations, visit www.derekprince.org.

Welcome to Our House!

We Have a Special Gift for You

It is our privilege and pleasure to share in your love of Christian books. We are committed to bringing you authors and books that feed, challenge, and enrich your faith.

To show our appreciation, we invite you to sign up to receive a specially selected **Reader Appreciation Gift**, with our compliments. Just go to the Web address at the bottom of this page.

God bless you as you seek a deeper walk with Him!

WE HAVE A GIFT FOR YOU. VISIT:

whpub.me/nonfictionthx

WHITAKER HOUSE